THINK

Microsoft® .NET

Bart A. DePetrillo

Think Microsoft® .NET

International Standard Book Number: 0-7897-2595-9

Library of Congress Catalog Card Number: 2001096099

Printed in the United States of America

First Printing: December 2001

05   04   03   02   4   3   2   1

A very special thank you to Jon Lasser, author of *Think Unix*, for his initial vision of the *Think* book concept.

Trademarks

Warning and Disclaimer

Associate Publisher
Dean Miller

Executive Editor
Candace Hall

Acquisitions Editor
Loretta L. Yates

Development Editor
Mark Cierzniak

Managing Editor
Thomas Hayes

Project Editor
Tricia S. Liebig

Copy Editor
Kezia Endsley

Indexer
Erika Millen

Proofreader
Jody Larsen

Technical Editor
Ankur Laroia

Team Coordinator
Cindy Teeters

Interior Designer
Maureen McCarty

Cover Designer
Anne Jones

Page Layout
Michelle Mitchell

Table of Contents

About the Author

 **Bart A. DePetrillo** has worked professionally in the computer software industry for the last nine years in a range of different positions and with various companies. After earning his Master of Computer Science from the Courant Institute of Mathematics at New York University he began working for the U.S. subsidiary of a leading German financial software company. Bart's career spanned from that of developer to Director of the New York office, where he worked for four years until becoming an independent consultant. In June of 2000 he and some of his former colleagues joined together to start newtelligence AG where he is responsible for content production, as well as international business development.

newtelligence AG has worked closely with Microsoft Germany to produce a readiness kit for .NET developers. The *Microsoft .NET Developer Readiness Toolkit* is a collection of 30 modules, each of which targets a specific area of .NET technology. The modules are designed for consultants and trainers to use to educate developers and get them up to speed on .NET. Each module is comprised of a presentation slide deck (PowerPoint) and speaker notes, both of which are distributable to clients to take home and for reuse and redelivery to customers. The content of the modules varies from overview to in-depth depending on the topic and many of the modules include sample source codes and references to other useful learning material. Of the 17 modules newtelligence AG produced, Bart authored or contributed to .NET Overview, XML, ADO.NET, HTTP, and .NET Framework Library. The other modules newtelligence AG authored include, but are not limited to C#, Visual Basic.NET, ASP.NET, Web Services Overview, Security, Context and Remoting, Reflection, and Managed C++.

Bart and newtelligence AG continue to produce customized content on .NET and BizTalk Server 2000 and present their material world-wide, including major conferences such as Microsoft TechEd 2000/2001, SIGS/101 XML One, and Microsoft Global Briefing. They also deliver onsite seminars, as well as host courses at their corporate headquarters.

Dedication

Thanks to my brilliant brother, Paolo, for advising me to enter this amazingly wonderful world of software. I cannot (and do not want to) imagine a different life!

Acknowledgments

Clemens F. Vasters for his support and our friendship, partnership, and history together; Achim Oellers and Joerg Freiberger for their dedication to this thing we call newtelligence—and of course for listening to my moans and groans; Bijan Javidi of Microsoft Germany for driving the Microsoft .NET Developer Tools Readiness Kit initiative; to the endless number of others that in various ways helped make this book possible; and lastly, but certainly not least, Jhoanna Bergande for putting up with me and the creation of this book!

I would like to give special acknowledgment to everyone that worked on the Microsoft .NET Developer Tools Readiness Kit. The "RK," as it is known amongst all that worked on it, was and continues to be a driving force in helping educate developers, consultants, and trainers on all the various aspects of .NET. It's modular composition (30 modules at last count) aptly covers topics including C#, Visual Basic .NET, ADO.NET, Web services, Context and Remoting, Reflection, and much, much more. Some of the material is publicly available at http://www.microsoft.com/germany/ms/msdnbiblio/DotNETRK/. While the material is in English, the page is in German.

Tell Us What You Think!

As the reader of this book, *you* are our most important critic and commentator. We value your opinion and want to know what we're doing right, what we could do better, what areas you'd like to see us publish in, and any other words of wisdom you're willing to pass our way.

As an Associate Publisher for Que, I welcome your comments. You can fax, e-mail, or write me directly to let me know what you did or didn't like about this book—as well as what we can do to make our books stronger.

Please note that I cannot help you with technical problems related to the topic of this book, and that due to the high volume of mail I receive, I might not be able to reply to every message.

When you write, please be sure to include this book's title and author as well as your name and phone or fax number. I will carefully review your comments and share them with the author and editors who worked on the book.

Fax: 317-581-4666

E-mail: feedback@quepublishing.com

Mail: Dean Miller
           Que
           201 West 103rd Street
           Indianapolis, IN 46290 USA

Introduction

What's Covered in This Book

Larry Ellison, CEO of Oracle, said, "We've had three major generations of computing: mainframes, client-server, and Internet computing. There will be no new architecture for computing for the next 1,000 years." I am certainly in no position to contest such an eminent figure of the software revolution. Mr. Ellison has guided the industry for many years at the helm of Oracle and his company has accomplished many positive things. After all, Oracle's main product line, its Oracle databases including the latest version Oracle 9i, are installed in companies worldwide.

Nonetheless, I do wonder what Mr. Ellison *really* thinks about Microsoft's .NET Platform. I would not venture to be so bold as to say that .NET is revolutionary. But putting it in Darwinist terms, it is undoubtedly a significant evolutionary step—perhaps even a leap! Yes, .NET does use the same old Internet technologies that have driven revenues of Oracle and other software companies through the roof and fueled an economic expansion in the United States not heralded in my lifetime. (I realize that given current economic data, things no longer look so rosy. However, economies *are* cyclical and the software industry will continue to make billions, regardless of the fact that, in comparison to the last five years, it might not seem so.) But more important to you perhaps, software will continue to be a driving force in making people more efficient.

.NET is wired with Internet technologies but it is also a new architecture for developing and delivering both the Web experience you know today as well as a whole new, more powerful component-based one. Perhaps Web services weren't invented by Microsoft corporation (Sun Microsystems has certainly mentioned some *similar* vision in the past), but Bill Gates and Company are undoubtedly going to be the first to bring a comprehensive version of this vision to fruition— and with elegance and ease of implementation!

Who Is This Book For?

If you are looking to learn the ins and outs of programming using the .NET Platform, I am sorry to disappoint you; I don't think this book is for you. If, however, you are an IT decision maker, a developer, or even a non-technical person looking to get a handle on the vision and how it might affect you, either directly or indirectly, *Think Microsoft.NET is* for you.

What's in *Think Microsoft.NET?*

Chapter 1: Types of Software Systems Today

Think Microsoft.NET begins by looking at the current state of software development and delivery. The types of software solutions that exist today, from desktop to Internet portal, are discussed in Chapter 1.

Chapter 2: Challenges of Software

Chapter 2 explores the challenges that software presents for both development organizations and the end-user with particular emphasis on the corporate customer. You will read how some development choices, such as the development tools and languages, are often not made for the reasons you might expect. Other development considerations are highlighted, including software delivery, stability, and maintenance.

Deploying software is addressed, with an emphasis on the corporate customer. The challenges to security and stability that installing new software presents is highlighted, which often center around software updates.

Together, these points will help you better appreciate .NET as you learn more about it in later chapters.

Chapter 3: Why .NET?

Once you have fleshed out all the *issues* of the status quo, the book embarks on answering the most basic question that even Microsoft has trouble conveying, what is .NET? Chapter 3 begins with the .NET vision, discusses its formidable promise, and then explains how .NET delivers on this promise. This chapter will also give you a solid introduction to the concept of Web services and provides some possible business scenarios for their use. The chapter also talks about Microsoft Hailstorm, a set of building block services to which companies and individuals can subscribe.

Chapter 4: What Is .NET?

The "what" of .NET is a short overview of what parts make-up the .NET Platform, including the .NET Framework, Visual Studio .NET, and the .NET enterprise servers.

Chapter 5: Introducing the Class Library

The .NET Framework is composed of several parts, of which the class library is arguably the most significant and is actually the same infrastructure upon which the .NET Platform was built. You will read about the various services that this library provides and learn some of its technical features. In addition to hearing about its data types and class support you will learn something about how the library is organized.

Chapter 6: Common Language Runtime

One of the more technical aspects of .NET by definition is the common language runtime, which is the engine that makes .NET solutions run. You will learn about the various components of the runtime including the common type system, the common language specification, the garbage collector, just-in-time compiling, security, and more.

Chapter 7: Web Services

Having had an introduction to Web services in Chapter 3, this chapter brings to light some of the technology behind the .NET services and points you to the right places to further your learning, if you are so inclined. More importantly to you as an information technology manager, the discussion addresses how .NET changes producing/consuming software.

Chapter 8: The Visual Studio .NET

Visual Studio .NET Enterprise Architecture Edition (EAE) is more than an upgrade to the Visual Studio tool suite. This new version does facilitate building traditional Windows applications using the new version of the Microsoft Foundation Classes (MFC) but it also enables you to build .NET applications, including Web services. Besides making it possible to program in any .NET language from scratch or using one of the numerous project templates, Visual Studio .NET EAE has a new, more intuitive user interface that aids you when building .NET solutions. You will learn about the interface and tools, and will get a glimpse of how the development environment facilitates producing Web services.

Chapter 9: Introducing .NET Enterprise Servers

Chapter 9 provides a brief overview of the .NET Enterprise Servers: BizTalk Server 2000, Exchange Server 2000, Host Integration Server 2000, Security and Acceleration Server 2000, SQL Server 2000, Application Center 2000, Commerce Server 2000, Mobile Information Server 2001, and SharePoint Portal Server 2001. The focus is highlighting the major features to give you a grasp of how you might utilize them for your solutions.

Chapter 10: Migration Paths—From Anywhere to .NET

This chapter explains some of the migration paths available to you. If you have Windows COM/COM+–based solutions, "Support for COM" in the .NET section will be of special interest. .NET provides support for "standard" C/C++ (for example, non-COM/COM+) based solutions as well. In "Support for C/C++" you learn about some basic techniques to continue using existing C/C++ code as you migrate to .NET. Lastly, "From VB 6 to VB.NET" highlights how the .NET team has tried to ease the transition for existing Visual Basic to the latest, improved version: Microsoft Visual Basic .NET.

Chapter 11: Summarizing the Key Benefits of .NET

The key benefits of .NET are highlighted in the Summary to help the ideas of .NET gel in your mind and aid you in deciding if and where to go next.

Although this book is *not* written for developers, you will have the chance to learn some technological facts and gain an understanding of .NET's parts from a comfortable cruising altitude of 40,000 feet. The goal is to make sure that by the book's end, you know and understand the .NET buzzwords and have a firm understanding of the pieces that make up the .NET Platform—so that you can take the lead when it comes to deciding if .NET is for you and your organization.

If you are still with me, this book is for you!

Introduction to .NET and the .NET Framework

1

Types of
Software
Systems
Today

Like some science fiction characters, today's software solutions assume different forms depending on the market they target. When aiming at the consumer and small business marketplace, the preferred shape is a familiar and somewhat innocuous desktop application. Shrink-wrapped desktop applications require onsite installation; which means it's done directly on the user's PC. Therefore, desired features must run directly from the user's machine.

In the larger business environment, the solutions often take on a slightly different form of client/server software. This requires installation on both the server and, in most cases, on the user machines. Lastly are the Internet solutions, which generally take the form of portal sites on the Web.

No matter which form the software application assumes, it is still at its heart just a service designed to solve a problem, whether it enables you to work more efficiently or empowers you to do in minutes some task that, prior to the advent of the computer, would have taken hours or days.

Unfortunately, it often seems that computers and software are, in astrological terms, born under the sign of Gemini—their behavior and benefit lean towards the erratic and multi-faceted! On the one side, the personal computer–software-technology team has increased productivity many times over (imagined only perhaps by George Orwell or Aldous Huxley), whereas on the other hand it has failed us miserably. Although it is a challenge to develop, deploy and use software today; it also seems impossible to live without it!

To understand what .NET is and what it offers, it makes sense to examine the landscape today. This chapter first looks at the more popular software design solutions currently in use, followed by the challenges these solutions present to software developers and users. Lastly, it explores how .NET addresses these issues and how it will alter the landscape—for the better.

Desktop Solutions

Desktop software is the most commonly deployed "service solution" in existence. It is a chameleon that takes many shapes, colors, and sizes depending on the service it is aimed to deliver. However, whatever form the desktop application assumes, a few of its characteristics remain constant, as described in the following sections.

Leveraging the Features of the OS

Desktop applications are designed specifically for the computer operating system (OS) on which they are meant to run. This empowers them to rely on the services or features of the OS, such as file management, Internet support, security, and the basic architectural design and philosophy of the OS.

An example of leveraging the operating system architecture as a service is how developers can design and implement a Windows application using the Component Object Model (COM/COM+). COM is a Windows-specific development model and technology that eases the development of reusable software components. By using COM components, developers can snap together functionality they previously developed or that was created by a third party. The COM technology also makes it possible to create software that can embed in or link to other software. For example, you can insert an Excel spreadsheet containing your financial projections for the month into a report you are writing using Word.

Note

In reality, the features and functionality that COM offers do not come free of work; COM is by no means easy to learn or apply and there is a significant learning curve to become proficient at it.

Unfortunately, every new generation of a software solution seems to require a faster computer to get the same performance. The truth of the matter, however, is that performance stagnation is the result of packing the solution with more powerful, processor intensive features that were not possible on last year's PC. For example, in 1995 the hottest, new *Wintel* (Windows-Intel-based) PCs were using Intel's cutting edge Pentium 133MHz CPU.

Just imagine trying to run some of today's software, with all the dynamic and processor-intensive features, on that "speed demon" of yesterday—I bet a snail comes to mind! Having developed software for many years, I realize that it's not a matter of no one having thought of these new features in 1995, but that it probably was not feasible to add such features back then because of the performance drain. This is how new features become reality—with time and advancements. With all this in mind, desktop applications are generally faster than other types of architectures for general use applications, such as productivity suites.

Tied and Bound to the OS

The flip side of designing a solution specifically for an OS is that the application is then tied and bound to that particular OS. If the solution is designed for Windows, it will not run on Linux, OS/2, MacOS, or some other system. For the average consumer, this is not an issue. Depending on which trade publication or newspaper article you read, it is estimated that between 80 and 90 percent of home users use a Microsoft Windows flavored OS (such as Windows 95, Windows 98, Windows Me, or Windows 2000). The corporate user, in contrast, uses a variety of OSes, ranging from Microsoft Windows to IBM AIX and everything in between, including the trendy open-source OS: Linux. In such a heterogeneous environment, deploying a solution that is bound to a specific OS can be restrictive or even unacceptable.

In later chapters, you'll learn more about today's challenges, and can move on and take a look at some of the existing desktop solutions, beginning with probably the most widely known productivity suite: Microsoft Office.

Microsoft Office

As you well know, Microsoft Office contains a myriad of different applications aimed at enhancing your productivity. These productivity services enable you, as the user, to perform word processing tasks, send and receive e-mail, create to-do lists, manage your calendar, create presentations, create spreadsheets, and perform a number of other tasks.

Microsoft Word, for instance, enables you to write simple letters or reports with what-you-see-is-what-you-get (WYSIWYG) text formatting. It also includes automated features, such as generating a table of contents for your book or document, and provides the means to perform mail merges using a document boiler-plate and a list of contacts. Furthermore, it contains built-in tools, such as a spell checker and grammar checker, that you can invoke on demand or, in later versions, provide real-time checking and feedback as you type.

Although all these bundled features are empowering, most people do not use all of them and certainly not all at once. The requirements of the casual home user are different from those of the business or power user. As a home user, you might create a spreadsheet to track your home inventory or basic expenses. Perhaps you might even use some of the reporting and graphing features in Microsoft Excel to get a better handle on where and how you are spending your money so you can better project future expenses. This is, however, a far cry from how you or some others might use Excel at work. If you create spreadsheets for work, it is possible that you create complicated formulas, such as for depreciating the value of inventory or for cost analysis.

The difference in uses for the same Excel application also apply to Word, Outlook, and the other applications in Microsoft Office. It is because Microsoft Office, and many other desktop applications, target a wide audience that they come packed with countless features; one solution must satisfy the demands of *every* user. (Granted, not all applications are designed for "general" use, but a good many are.)

Some Negative Aspects of Desktop Applications

Although each successive version of any given desktop application includes additional features; many of them are not aimed at the common user but are niche features that address the needs of a segment of the overall market. Although the users who utilize these features praise their introduction, everyone else scratches their head in wonderment and sometimes in frustration, usually because these new features tend to make the application less intuitive and more unwieldy. To drive the point home, if you use Windows 2000 or Microsoft Office 2000, you will notice that the menus need not show every menu item but include an arrow as the last item. Clicking this arrow expands the menu choices to display all available options, not just the most recently used. This feature is actually a user interface (UI) enhancement to Windows to address the fact that showing all available options simply overwhelms most users.

The explosion of readily available features has introduced what is known in the computer field as bloatware. Installation sizes range from large to huge in both the massive amount of hard drive space required to house the solutions and in the amount of computer memory (RAM) required to run them. To drive this point home, I have switched to my task manager and checked the amount of memory used by Word 2000 at this time—a whopping 22,164KB! That is over half the RAM that computer systems came with only a few short years ago! In reality, the reason that so much hard drive space and RAM is consumed is because of the development environment of today, which .NET addresses with such things as Web services (more on that later).

Although resource capacity grows with every successive version of an application, performance is the primary victim. Those of us who hinge on paranoia often wonder if bloatware is really just a conspiracy to drive folks to upgrade their PCs. In reality, given today's development models, the burgeoning size of desktop applications is an unwanted and unintended side affect.

To their credit, some of the more recent desktop applications, such as Microsoft Office 2000, permit more fine-grained feature selection during installation, saving time and hard disk space. However, if you choose not to install a set of features until you need them, the application will then whine until you pop in your installation CD and install whatever you selected. That might be okay if you are a home user and the CD is handy, but if this happens at work, more likely than not it means you have to call your IT support to come to your rescue—which takes precious time from both your schedule and that of the IT department.

"Does it have to be this way?" is not that simple a question to address.

No, it no longer has to be the way it is today and you will learn how .NET offers to change the situation later. First, however, take a look at another popular architecture—client/server—that's used primarily in the business environment. It addresses this and a few other issues that desktop applications do not.

Client/Server Solutions

The easiest way to think of the client/server software architecture is to imagine a desktop application broken into logical pieces and distributed throughout a network of computers. The rationale behind such a design is not important at the moment; trust that software built this way is done rationally and has its particular benefits, some of which you'll learn about in the coming section.

The client/server model was born from two merging demands. First, as the personal computer became more powerful in the late 80s and early 90s, corporations began adopting it as a lower-cost solution to low-end business processing. Essentially, the PC took on the same displacing role that mini-computers had taken against their larger, much more expensive brethren, the mainframes. Companies viewed the PC as a means to make their employees more efficient and flexible than was economically viable with minis or mainframes.

In addition to running the shrink-wrapped desktop productivity applications, corporate information technology (IT) departments, as well as software consulting companies, began creating desktop applications specifically geared to solving business processes utilizing these relatively cheap PC platforms.

As the PC evolved and inundated the market, IT departments and hardware companies came to realize that while the personal computer empowered each person to do more than was previously possible with the hosted dumb terminals, the need for centralized processing of data (using terms loosely here) would not vanish. However, technology managers and manufacturers both realized that the Intel computer chips, which were driving the corporate PC revolution and the surrounding hardware, had sufficient performance to make it possible for the likes of Compaq to forge a new category of computer: the PC server.

Note

The "PC" in PC server is used only to differentiate these Intel-based computer servers from the pre-Intel based servers. "PC servers" are essentially just souped-up PCs. Granted, PC manufacturers in this market have always added hardware optimized to handle the task at hand, but the basic design and certainly the roots of the server lie with the vanilla desktop personal computers.

Designed not for an individual employee but as a shared resource accessible by multiple employees, the PC servers sat in the back rooms of IT departments. Initially, these machines were used for simple centralized tasks such as storing and accessing company files and data (what became known as file servers), acting as print servers, authenticating users on the corporate network and, in time, hosting a few small commonly accessible applications. Somewhere along the evolutionary path, software developers (including the corporate IT staffs) came up with the idea of taking the host-terminal model of the previous computing era and evolving it.

The idea was simply to alter the hosting model by replacing the dumb terminals with the already deployed "really smart terminals" (compared to dumb terminals, personal computers even in the late 1980s were Einsteins). The idea was simple: leverage the processing power that the client side of the host model now possessed.

Using PCs and servers had a cost advantage over the mainframes and minicomputers. Also, by utilizing the processing power of both the server and desktop client PCs, developers could create more robust, user-friendly, and efficient solutions than previously possible. Client/server computing was born.

Benefits of Client/Server Computing

The following list outlines some of the benefits of client/server solutions.

- **More for less**—Many benefits to client/server (C/S) computing exist over the traditional hosted or standalone desktop application models. As mentioned, companies can utilize lower-cost computers to achieve the same task.

  Many companies introduced PCs because their processing power and available software (cheap relative to custom mainframe) provided more bang for the buck. This added employee-side (read: client-side) processing power is what developers used to create a new breed of solutions not previously possible at the same price point.

- **Breaking it all down**—Furthermore, application developers can divide solutions into more manageable parts. As with the dumb terminal to mainframe design, the client machine provides a user interface to the solution; however, unlike with dumb terminals the PC-based clients have much more processing power. Therefore the PC-based terminal offers usability gains through a much richer user interface and, unlike dumb terminals, can perform business processing.

- **Centralized information storage**—While processing in the client-server model is distributed, information storage is centralized. The server stores the data and acts as a coordinator for accessing and modifying information. This minimizes information redundancy and aids in keeping data consistent, even when multiple users/clients are working with it.

- **Maintenance**—From development and maintenance standpoints, the client/server architecture makes things arguably easier. Generally speaking, the client is easy to implement; its tasks are broken into smaller, simpler tasks that, although imbued with logic, are more mechanical in nature. It is for these reasons that the client side is often implemented using rapid application development (RAD) tools, such as Microsoft Visual Basic, Borland Delphi, and Borland C++ Builder ().

The server side, in contrast, is responsible for coordinating all information to and from its clients. Furthermore, it must process this information in additional ways that are often more processor-intensive. These are but some of the many reasons that server components are difficult and costly to implement.

As such, the separation of business logic from the user interface can make updating a client/server solutions easier; the collateral impact of changes is minimized.

• **Security**—Because the client/server model moves information off the desktop and is centralized it makes securing data far easier. The server is often securely locked away, which prevents intentional tampering, unintentional accidents, unauthorized access, or surprise interruptions, which can happen when the server is inadvertently turned off by the cleaning staff.

In sum, the general design behind client/server software is that the common, processor-intensive services that can logically be centralized are hosted on the PC server and those less intensive, uncommon, or user-specific features find their way to the desktop PC. This enables people to produce more robust, manageable, and efficient solutions that gain in performance through a divide-and-conquer architecture.

Drawbacks to Client/Server Computing

Although client/server computing has many benefits, it also has disadvantages.

• **Complicated to implement**—Software development is about breaking a problem into pieces, making it easier to solve. To leverage the benefits of distributed processing the design of client server solutions often becomes complicated. This contradicts the earlier statement that they are easier to implement. Recall, there is a client and server side to this equation. Numerous issues including processing and data synchronization between clients and servers must be addressed depending on the solution architecture.

• **Costly**—Distributed computing is inherently more complicated and therefore requires more highly trained/experienced developers and architects. Obviously this raises production costs.

• **Longer production cycles**—The increased complexity again rears its head because the more complicated a solution the more time it takes to realize. This also increases the cost of the project.

The Internet Solution

Some view life as a circle. If you examine the software evolution from hosted application to desktop application to client/server application and now to the Internet application, you become aware that software is coming full circle. The Internet is after all the grandest, most host-centric system ever conceived. The Web browser is a marginally smarter client than the dumb terminal, relegated to rendering graphics and the UIs of client/server and desktop applications, but performing little to no business processing. Browsers instead rely almost completely on the Internet servers to which they connect. Okay, to be fair, Web-based applications can and often do perform some client-side processing using JScript and Dynamic HTML (DHTML). However, except for filling out an information request form that validates some of the data (such as verifying that the customer's name and address were entered or the entered date is valid), most processing is performed on the server side.

Note

JScript, JavaScript, and ECMAScript are more or less the same language sharing a common heritage. ECMAScript is the standardization of Netscape's JavaScript and Microsoft's JScript. If you are interested in learning more about ECMAScript visit www.ecma.org. For more information on DHTML, check out www.w3c.org.

These scripting languages are light-weight programming languages used by Web developers to perform processing on a Web page from the browser (the client side). However, more often than not, business logic isn't executed with JScript and the Dynamic HyperText Markup Language (DHTML). Instead, it's used for user interface-related tasks, such as creating dynamic navigation trees or pop-up context-sensitive windows to aid the user.

Thinking of the Web in universal terms, the "big-bang" happened around 1993 and spread outward at near lightspeed. In the beginning, the Web was a world of information that was magnificently useful but static. Web pages contained few graphics and the idea of dynamic pages with animations and sound was nothing more than a dream. As the Web became more popular and developed into common medium, corporations took note and at an increasingly rapid pace began publishing their presence starting around 1995. It was during the corporate push that the Web started to become more interactive. The corporate invasion (as many in academia view this period of transition from the Web's birth as a research tool to commercial use) started a demand for dynamic, user friendly and engaging pages. The result was that browser manufacturers, such as Microsoft and Netscape, began competing to supply the corporate demands, introducing features into their browsers in a breakneck upgrade pace that lead to sophisticated browsers of today.

As you know from the recently belabored dot-com revolution, during this time many companies were born whose existence orbited solely around the Internet. This was the beginning of what became "the portal wars" between Yahoo!, Excite, Lycos, and AltaVista in the years to follow.

Taking a step back from the front lines for a moment, the idea of a portal really came into existence as a result of browser designers creating the default Web page that's called up when users start their browsers. Yahoo! and most of the other contenders were originally conceived solely as simple search engines or directories to help Web surfers find Web sites of interest. The need for help finding sites in 1994 and 1995 was, in my opinion, even more of a necessity than today because, in its infancy, the Web was dominated by educators and personal sites. Today you can enter just about any word of interest surrounded by www. and .com and find a site of interest. For this reason, it made practical sense to make a search page the default page of many users.

Returning to the battle once again, when these search sites became companies during the initial public offering (IPO) mania of the late 1990s, they needed to produce revenues, primarily through ad dollars. For this reason, becoming a Web surfer's default page became the prime objective of these search companies.

It did not take long for the competitors to realize that the greatest power of the Internet—the capability to jump from one source of information to another at a click—was also their biggest threat. The harsh reality: Web customers were viciously loyal but only for about an Internet minute. Logically, the second field of battle was fought in finding ways to make surfers not only continue to use their sites as the default page but in getting users to stay at the site as long as possible. It is from this idea of maintaining surfers' attentions that the term "stickiness" was coined.

The main strategy employed by these warring Web sites to create stickiness was to offer various services to surfers. The portal wars present an interesting business case study, but aren't within the scope of this book.

Today's Web Services: Passport

Microsoft provides its own preview of .NET services with its creation of Microsoft Passport. Understanding the where, what, and why behind Passport requires revisiting Yahoo! and the other Web portal services.

Almost every Web site today offers some kind of personalization. This ranges between content and layout customization, such as in My Yahoo! and The Wall Street Journal Interactive Edition, to managing online payment preferences. The one aspect common to all personalization efforts is that you, the Web surfer, need to identify yourself so that your preferences can be saved and restored as you come and go.

Technically, enabling a Web site to store user identities and preferences is rather straightforward. The development team creates a registration page that enables the users to designate a username and password, which the site uses to uniquely identify and authorize each user. A username is analogous to a customer number, serving as an identifier. More often than not, the registration page also requests varying degrees of personal information, such as mail address, e-mail address, and phone number, some of which are later used to personalize content and advertisements.

From the user standpoint, setting up personalization can prove rather time consuming. Most sites require you to register and create a user name and password that becomes your identity. Because this identity process is first come first serve, often your choice of username is taken and you must choose another. One challenge is remembering which name/password combination you used on each site.

One of the key concepts behind the Passport service is that it manages information that is uniquely yours. Conceptually, it's like the wallet in your back pocket or a purse: it stores personal information such as your mailing address, phone number, and birth date. It can securely store your credit card and other sensitive information (see Figure 1.1), and it can manage the various username/password combinations you have with different Web sites.

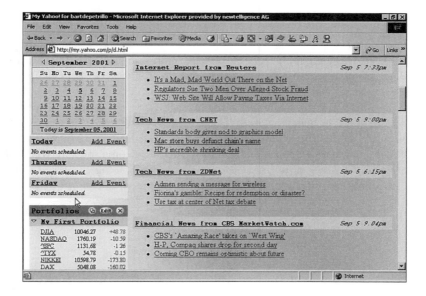

Figure 1.1

Microsoft Passport wallet service page stores your credit card information securely.

Essentially, it aims to make your Web surfing experience as effortless as possible by alleviating the need to re-enter or remember information that is unique to you. For instance, if you purchase an item from a site that utilizes Passport, you do not have to retype your name, credit card number, expiration date, and billing address every time you shop at another site. Passport conveys this information to the site without requiring you to get actively involved. This saves you time and aggravation; however, Passport only releases the information you authorize. Passport is an example of a non-.NET Web service.

Note

If you are interested in seeing a complete list of e-tailers that use Passport, point your browser to http://www.passport.com/Directory.

Passport, however useful now, is mostly built on yesterday's Web or proprietary technologies. It does not leverage the open technology solutions that underlie .NET, including XML, SOAP, and UDDI. These services enable Web sites to more easily integrate; this in turn is what will make Web services ubiquitous.

Summary

There are many different types of software solutions in use today. Each has its respective positive and negative aspects. The desktop variety offers you personalized power that revolutionized business. Client/server solutions further leveraged the power of the desktop while increasing manageability and security all while delivering cost and user benefits. You have read that the current trend is to revisit the past and improve it with the Internet technologies available today. Microsoft Passport provides you with a good indication of what at least some software will evolve into. You will learn more about Web services in the coming chapter, as well as how they address the various challenges facing development today.

Challenges
of Software

The development of software solutions is far from a trivial task. It takes an ever-increasing amount of effort, especially for business solutions. As you might very well be aware, each endeavor requires analysis, planning, and implementation.

This chapter does not delve into what you need to do for software production; there is no best-practices analysis presented here. There are plenty of great books on software design and project management, and these issues are out of the scope of this book.

Note

Looking for a great software project management book that's appropriate *for anyone involved in a project?* Check out Steve McConnell's *Software Project Survival Guide* (ISBN: 1-57231-621-7). To his credit, he also did a fabulous job at exploring and exposing the rapid application development process in *Rapid Development: Taming Wild Software Schedules* (ISBN: 1-55615-900-5).

This chapter presents some of the *many* challenges that software presents at various stages in its lifecycle. It does not strive to fully explore the complexity of these issues—although you do examine some of them—or to discover the solutions to the problems that face the development teams today. This chapter also doesn't serve as a guide for information technologists about how to navigate the potential mine-fields of deploying and using software solutions in a corporate environment. The objective here is to raise some of the more common issues in order to augment the advantages of developing and deploying .NET-based solutions as you learn about the Microsoft .NET vision and architecture.

Challenges for the Development Organization

The development organization, or any developer for that matter, faces a myriad of challenges during the software cycle, from development, delivery, and continuing throughout the maintenance process.

How the Operating System (OS) Is Chosen

The developer or organization historically attacks a problem by first asking "What is the target platform?" The answer might be one of several possibilities: Microsoft Windows 95, Windows 98, Windows Millennium Edition, Windows NT, or Windows 2000; the Apple Macintosh; Unix (any given flavor); or even *a* Web browser (such as Internet Explorer, Netscape/AOL, or Opera).

Two questions that might come to the forefront of your consciousness are:

- Why *a* target platform?
- Why not the best platform *for* the solution (such as the one that offers the most complementary or required features)?

Using some basic common sense, the answer to the second question is simple. If the solution solves the users' problems it doesn't matter if they are not using the most efficient operating system (OS). Although it might prove more difficult to develop the solutions, at least they will run on the target market's PCs!

The answer to the first question is a bit different because there are numerous types of operating systems but few tools that provide one solution for the multiple systems used by potential customers. The reason for such a dearth of cross-language and cross-OS tools and methods is that it is difficult to create such tools.

Although many of the functions that each OS performs appear to be the same on the surface, what happens behind the scenes is a different matter all together! For example, if you were given a clean sheet of paper and a pencil and a picture, you would undoubtedly draw your picture in a different way than your spouse or colleague—even though the result might look exactly the same. You are an individual with your own ideas of how to arrive at the goal, just like the engineers of OSes from different (and competing) companies.

To hammer the idea home, consider a task such as saving a file. In Microsoft Windows or on the Apple Macintosh, you select a *File* menu and then choose *Open, Save or Save As*, depending on your intent. To open a file, the program shows a dialog box with a graphical representation of your hard drive and allows you to navigate through the file structure to find the file you want to open. Behind the scenes, OS-specific commands are sent and received. For instance, displaying the existing documents and folders in the dialog box requires issuing some kind of "give me the directory" command. Although each OS contains logically similar methods to perform such a task, the actual command or even set of commands required are distinctly different; no commonly accepted methods exist between OSes.

Certainly, you can at least begin to understand and appreciate the challenge of developing a solution for *every* possible computer operating system—it's daunting! Now, consider that the tools required for creating cross-platform software are themselves software—the Catch-22 sort of jumps out at you.

For this reason, part of the market analysis when developing a software solution focuses on determining the platforms the target audience uses. When such analysis determines that one OS is dominant, most companies tend to choose that OS as the only target platform, even when the margin of the lead isn't great. Take the following example in which the target market for "Solution X" is comprised of three OSes with the distribution shown in Figure 2.1.

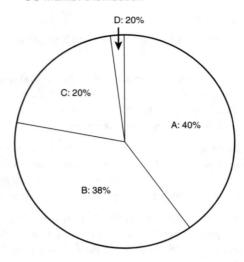

OS Market Distribution

D: 20%

C: 20%

A: 40%

B: 38%

Figure 2.1

Example of distribution of market share among different OSes.

Now, although OS A is used by 45% of potential customers, choosing to develop a solution for A means that the developers can *at best* gain only 45% of the market. Presuming they already have competitors in this market, their ability to realize 45% will, in all probability, be unachievable. Not a very inviting picture is it?

Altering the scenario somewhat, imagine the distribution in Figure 2.2, which might bring some more-or-less real markets to mind.

From this data, it's a rather easy choice. But what if segment A is already comprised of three vendors producing 10 solutions that compete with the one you are about to create, whereas segments B, C, and D have little to no potential competition?

If this were your software company, wouldn't you prefer to produce one solution that targets some combination of A, B, C, and D, if not all of them?

On the other hand, if you are not involved in software development but are a user, it is reasonable to expect that you do not give a hoot about any of this, as long as you happen to be in the market that is best served. But this *is* the point: if software companies are able to easily develop for multiple markets or OSes, it increases their chances of success, at least in terms of revenues earned. In the end, this means they will have more money to maintain, extend, and support their—your—solutions. Now that is in everyone's interest!

OS Market Distribution

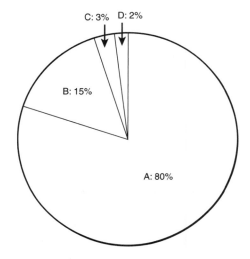

Figure 2.2

Example of distribution of market share among different OSes.

OS Limits Choice of Development Languages and Tools

Tying into the OS-centric development model are the actual development languages and tools. As mentioned, software tools face the same cross-platform obstacles as other software. So, after the OS of the target customer is discovered and a decision is made to proceed with development, the development team must choose one or more languages and tools to use in building the solution.

In an ideal world, the development team would choose the best language or languages for the solution. For instance, in building a client/server or Internet or intranet application, they might choose Java for the server side, because of its portability and ease of development, whereas on the client they prefer to use Visual Basic. In this scenario, assume that the solution targets financial institutions whereby 60% of the servers and user machines use Solaris and 40% use some flavor of Windows. Also assume that developers prefer to use Microsoft Visual Basic as the development language and tool for the client-side application. A hindrance that impedes this path is that Microsoft Visual Basic 6 runs only on Windows. In the end, this means that the development team must either use a different solution for all client-side applications—one that targets both Solaris and Windows—or use two tools—which means developing two client-side solutions that do the same thing. Back to the cross-platform quagmire.

Because some development languages are really only an extension of a tool—they are essentially a proprietary language available only with the tool with which they were invented—the best tool choice is often not possible. If you think Visual Basic version 6 is the best client-side development language for your solution but you have to target Solaris—too bad, you have to find and use something else.

Note

Although Java is mentioned here, it is *not* a standardized language. Sun Microsystems invented it and maintains control over it, just as Microsoft does with Visual Basic. The fact that Java can be made to run on multiple systems does not make it any less proprietary.

Now consider a "standardized" language: C++. C++ was invented by Bijan Straustrupp and was standardized by the American National Standards Institute (ANSI) and International Standards Institute (ISO). The standard defines the grammar and syntax of the language and provides the information required by tool vendors to implement language compilers. As such, software vendors have all the details they need to implement the language on different operating systems (which means they can produce development tools that compile C++ programs to run on any given OS).

Even with a common standard, very few *compilers* (the tool that takes a C++ program and turns it into an application) target more than one OS. Microsoft Visual C++ and Borland C++ Builder target Windows, Gnu C/C++ targets multiple Unix and Linux varieties, and MetroWerks CodeWarrior targets the MacOS. MetroWerks CodeWarrior and Sybase Watcom C/C++ (which now only lives on in the open source world as OpenWatcom—www.openwatcom.org) are the only mass-market C++ compilers that target multiple operating systems—not just different flavors of the same OS.

CodeWarrior lets developers use the same tool to produce MacOS, Windows, and Palm OS solutions. Furthermore, when you develop in vanilla C++, you can't leverage the OS-specific features.

Unfortunately, two obstacles to leveraging the OS via its application programming interfaces (APIs) exist. First, the operating system APIs might not be in C++. Second, even if they are in C/C++, it is unwieldy to do application development directly by calling the APIs. For this reason, most vendors create "frameworks" that consolidate OS APIs into essentially proprietary programming models. Sometimes in creating these frameworks, tool vendors will actually extend the underlying programming language to better integrate and or offer additional features. Borland's C++ Builder, for instance, introduced the property keyword into C++ to complement their development concept, which includes creating object properties. This shows that even a standard language is not so standard in the real world.

Software is simply the expression of logic and functionality of a specific language that is transformed into an application. So why is cross-platform development so difficult? Giving credit where it is due, the Java language and its corresponding platform is a good first attempt at achieving cross-platform development. As you will learn, .NET, has learned from the positive and negative aspects of Java, to fully achieve what Java endeavored—and *much* more.

Are You Experienced? (Language and Tool Experience)

Essentially these frameworks are an effort to make development easier, but in reorganizing the OS APIs, the vendors create their own programming library with its own APIs and attributes. The tradeoff for developers is that coding becomes easier only after they conquer the sometimes-steep learning curve needed to master the framework. Unfortunately, the knowledge gained is only applicable to the particular framework and, although the concepts and layout are often similar, there is a significant learning curve between tools.

For those of you who are loyal Java fans, the same is true of this "write once run anywhere" language. Sun Microsystems has essentially published the Java language reference and SDK in the public domain in order to make Java *appear* non-proprietary and open. In reality, however, Sun has continued to retain control over the Java language and requires vendors to sign licensing agreements for commercial use that include restrictions on extending or modifying the language.

No Turning Back

Harking back to the OScentricity of development (meaning it focuses around one particular operating system) there are huge opportunities and financial costs associated with developing solutions today. Obviously, the fact that it is often feasible to target only one platform per solution (one application per platform) means foregoing the opportunity of serving potential customers using other OSes. It also means that after development begins, should the organization realize that it needs to target another OS, the work involved is prohibitively expensive—often so much so that changing OSes means starting over! In other words, after the kayak enters the rapids, there is little hope of going back!

Distribution: Production and Delivery

The next challenge comes after companies have successfully produced a solution: delivering it to customers. Production and delivery are two separate steps, however, because they are so intertwined, they are discussed together.

There are two traditional methods of software distribution: compact disk (CD) and floppy disk. The third method is via electronic delivery (eDelivery). eDelivery is likely the most promising technique in the long-term, but currently lacks a sufficient infrastructure to make it prevalent. The following sections look at a few of the issues that arise when choosing any one of the aforementioned delivery methods.

Logistics and Planning for Delivery: CDs and Floppies

The fact that using CDs or floppy disks requires the use of a physical medium, and therefore production of software on the medium, is the crux of the distribution challenge. Because both these mediums face more or less the same challenges, the dominant CD media is used to illustrate the point.

Long before the software solution is finished, the company must coordinate to make sure all the pertinent issues are addressed so the product can actually be delivered. The steps to producing a solution on CD includes much more than simply developing the solution and recording it; there is artwork to do, inserts to create, packaging to perform. When everything is finalized it must be shipped to the distributor, retail outlet, or directly to the customer.

This is the "off-the-shelf" scenario. Software can also be distributed at the enterprise level, whereby it's installed and configured by or with the help of consultants. In this event, physical delivery might require the consultant to deliver the solution in person.

eDelivery

The electronic delivery (eDelivery) method is superior in several ways. For starters, there are very little costs involved in packaging the deliverable. There are no CDs to burn and no CD packaging to design and print. Besides the savings in physical production costs, fewer people are needed to produce this solution because less coordination and planning are necessary. The difference in the required levels of involvement translates into time saved.

Another, perhaps more troublesome, aspect is that although you can trust software you download from established software companies, the same cannot be said for software eDelivered from other lesser-known (or unknown) sources.

Currently, "stop gap" solutions exist, such as Verisign Athenticode, to give users an additional sense of security, but most of these solutions are still based on taking someone's word that the program is safe. The Authenticode model relies on Verisign—an independent third-party certificate provider—to verify that a program comes from the stated company. This process is not fool proof. In fact, a Verisign employee was duped to giving out Microsoft Authenticode certificates to a non-Microsoft employee!

At the end of the day, it is the user who must address the authenticity and security challenges because there is no development model or means for developers to mark their software with an authenticator. Even with packaged software, there is no way that non-.NET developers can encode a description that reliably informs the system what the code does or the degree of system level access it needs. For instance, will it need access to the local disk for any reason, perhaps to write or read files? Will it require certain system services? A development and runtime platform that lets developers provide a means to authenticate their application, as well as programmatically request varying degrees of security permission is in demand. This is especially true when talking about downloaded applications or services delivered via Internet—.NET addresses this.

The last challenge of deployment is the by-product of development. As mentioned in Chapter 1, today's software development model tends to deliver monolithic solutions. Providing enough features to satisfy a cross segment of the population requires packaging all the available features in the solution. This necessity is what makes today's solutions *so* large—and therefore often impractical to delivery via Internet—imagine downloading Microsoft Word or Corel WordPerfect with a 56Kbps modem! Although DSL and cable modems are becoming increasingly available in the US, the rate of adoption of these high-bandwidth solutions is much lower in the rest of the world.

Stability

Stability is an interesting challenge to developers. It encompasses not only each line of code but how the code interacts with other solutions.

> Abandon All Hope Ye Who Enters Here
>
> —Dante, *Inferno*

If you are a Windows computer user, you might not have even known it, but you have had your mind scorched by DLL compatibility issues, known colloquially as "DLL Hell." Did you ever install a new application on your PC and then notice that some of your software has stopped working or crashes intermittently for no apparent reason? How about getting weird behavior after upgrading a piece of software? Did your Web browser start crashing randomly after installing a download manager for your browser? If you answered "yes" to any of these scenarios, you have had the pleasure of experiencing system pollution side effects—also known as "DLL Hell."

The problem that arises is that previously installed, running software might not work with the newly installed version because of DLL incompatibilities.

Technically this is not a bug, although it has the same effect as one! As you might know from experience, these incompatibilities are difficult to find and resolve. Unfortunately, a good solution to this problem, using today's systems and shared by both developers and consumers, does not exist.

For this reason, development teams must not only test their solutions for internal errors but must also test the compatibility of their solutions with today's popular software—or at least against the software they expect is deployed in the market they are targeting. Certainly it will not help the organization if the software is stable when running alone but breaks all other programs when installed in the client environment! In a phrase, "test, test, test." Of course, it is all but impossible to test against every possible configuration. Without new system architectures, however, this is often the only viable means of ensuring real-world stability.

The .NET platform addresses this issue head on by casting off the notion of shared system DLLs that each solution modifies to deliver specialized "common" features. As you will learn, each .NET applications or version of an application is self contained in what is known as an assembly.

Another major issue when developing stable software comes from handling, or mishandling, computer memory. If your computer experience dates back to Windows 3.1 or even Windows 95, you *are* familiar with the dreaded "General Protection Fault" (GPF) error message. This was the death knoll for your OS. The reality was that a program mishandled memory access in some way and destabilized the computer as a result.

In later versions of Windows, the error did not disappear but the message did; the GPF became an "Access Violation at reference…" Along with the change in the message, Windows was able to (mostly) recover from this type of error—in the case of Windows 98. Windows 2000 can normally survive intact through such incidents. The root of the problem is a development issue that has hardly improved over the years. The problem is that software requires memory to store and retrieve data. The program code is responsible for requesting, assigning, and returning the memory. Therein lies the problem; the process mostly relies on the developer handling memory properly, which opens it up to human error.

Generally, memory is allocated to the program in one place, passed around, and used in different places. Somewhere along the line, the memory is *unallocated* (meaning that it is given back to the OS for use by other programs). However, if some other part of the same program maintains a reference to this released memory (it isn't informed of the fact that the memory has been freed from use) and attempts to use it anyway (that's where the term "access violation" comes from), problems ensue.

The converse of this problem, known as a memory leak, occurs when a developer forgets to release memory back to the OS, but releases (or never again uses) the references to the memory. Thus, like a leaking bucket that loses a drop at a time until eventually it is empty, memory that is forgotten this way slowly adds up until there is no more available memory for any programs to use. Thankfully, you can restart your computer to get the memory back.

In contrast to access violations, memory leaks are harder to discover. Luckily, memory leaks do not have a profound effect on your *personal* computer—with 64MB to 128MB of memory (RAM) on today's systems and the comparatively small size of leaks in today's software, you will seldom notice that your RAM is draining. For server-based software, on the other hand, memory leaks *are* significant. Unlike personal computers, servers are designed and intended to be turned on and forgotten—for months if not years—which means they are rarely rebooted.

.NET also addresses the challenges of memory management. The common language runtime, as you will learn in Chapter 6, "Common Language Runtime," frees developers from the need to manage memory, letting them concentrate on building features.

Maintenance

Maintenance has proven itself the Achilles heel of software, often requiring significant updates to the existing version. Given the current development, production, and delivery methods, maintenance updates often require delivering an entirely new version. As you might imagine, maintenance also introduces all the aforementioned headaches. The main development shortcoming is that there is no good, commonly accepted way to version solutions. Certainly on Windows, componentization of solutions (creating the solution using different and distinct components) is possible using such technologies as the Microsoft Component Object Model (COM), however versioning in COM does not permit what is known as side-by-side deployment. So, if a development organization creates a new version of a commonly used COM component and deploys it with their update, the new component will replace the older one. This makes sense logically, however, such a replacement might result in decreased stability.

Practically speaking, it makes sense to permit both versions of the same component to reside on the system so that only software designed and tested for the new component will use it, whereas the previous solutions can continue to use their version. Unfortunately, today's systems are incapable of doing this. Windows cannot run multiple versions of the same COM component; a component update will always replace the older version.

As mentioned, in .NET each solution is packaged and delivered as an assembly. Because no COM/COM+ components need updating, software maintenance does not have the problems it has today. Additionally, .NET addresses software versioning head-on and makes it possible to deploy different versions of a solution on the same machine.

Challenges of the Corporate Customer

Having learned the trials that developers must confront when developing their solutions, it's time now to examine how their customers face similar challenges. Although the focus of this section is on the corporate customer, the average consumer experiences most of these issues, albeit on a different scale.

Deployment

Today, the corporate customer, or more specifically the network administration team, bares the burden of deploying software. Because solutions more often than not come on a physical medium, combined with the fact that in most organizations the user is not authorized to install software, deployment requires that someone from the administrative team walk over to every machine on which the software needs to be installed, sit down, and run the installation.

Today many solutions, such as Microsoft Office, have a network installation routine whereby the administrator can install the application on a single server and configure an "installation point" so that client machines can run a setup routine from the installation point. Although this takes less time because the software is physically loaded from the media once, often the installation process still requires that an administrator perform the client setup.

Although pulling software from the server in this way does have advantages over walking around to each machine with CD in hand, it is certainly not the best method you can probably dream up. In a small office, this "pull" model may not present much work, but imagine a large company with thousands of computers. Because of the enormity of the task, it is no wonder that many IT teams perform staged rollouts. Employees are grouped by priority and then the solution is implemented in stages, one group at a time.

Stability and Security

Keeping the burden of the pull model in mind, consider some of the issues discussed in the context of developers, such as interoperability with other applications. For these reasons, you must address some basic questions before deploying any solution:

- From where does the software come?
- Is it stable?
- Can the installation potentially create a security breach?
- Can the installation potentially destabilize the system or other applications?

Unfortunately, administrators sit on the other end of the table from developers today. Although developers can only test thoroughly to answer these questions, administrators can only do the same to make sure the developers have adequately done their part! In the end, both the developers and customers must perform extensive quality assurance (QA) testing.

Maintenance

Maintenance is another great undertaking. A maintenance update, even one that fixes known bugs, requires the same diligence and involvement that deploying a new solution requires. After all, there is no way to know how these updates will affect the system. Often, a maintenance release doesn't update a few components of the software, but completely replaces it! If you work for a large company, this might be why you are not using the latest and greatest version of your word processor or e-mail client. Without proper evaluation, permitting workers to use the latest versions can be tantamount to negligence!

Summary

Today's software solutions present a myriad of challenges to both developers and customers. Most all these issues are rooted in the operating system architecture. It defines the rules by which developers must adhere when producing solutions and how software interacts with the OS and other applications once deployed. Developers are hampered by the tool-language-OS choice and the lack of cross platform or cross-language support. In the decade old COM world there is no support for side-by-side deployment of component versions causing developer and customer headaches. The lack of automatic memory management in most development environments degrades stability and introduces application errors. And the absence of adequate programmatic security is a hindrance. These are fundamental issues that you face today—and that .NET addresses.

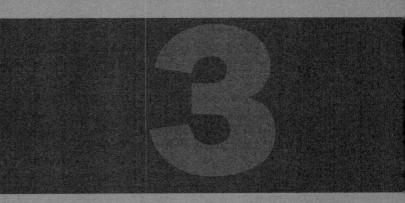

Why .NET?

In this chapter, you will gain a broad view of .NET by learning more about the vision behind it. This chapter provides an overview of .NET, including its vision and promise. Once you have this in mind, I expect your cranial cogs will start understanding how .NET addresses the challenges set forth in Chapter 2, "Challenges of Software." The opportunities .NET affords should begin to become clearer. The chapter begins with the vision and the promise of .NET.

The Vision and Promise

.NET, as the name suggests, is Internet-oriented. It is not some technology or framework that has been rewired and "Internet-enabled." If you come from pre-Internet COM days, this is not COM repackaged into ActiveX as an Internet solution. Nor is .NET like Citrix WinFrame or MetaFrame products, which promise to let you run and manage applications over the wire as if it were a native solution. Based on the Internet and for the Internet, the .NET architecture is a first-class Internet citizen.

The manner in which .NET achieves its ability to integrate seamlessly with the Web is because it is built using the same open and commonly accepted standards that grease the cogs of the Internet machine, including:

- The Hypertext Transfer Protocol (HTTP)
- The eXtensible Markup Language (XML)
- The Simple Object Access Protocol (SOAP)
- The HyperText Markup Language (HTML)
- TCP/IP
- Universal Description Discovery Integration (UDDI)
- Web Service Description Language (WSDL)
- Simple Mail Transfer Protocol (SMTP)
- WebDAV
- Multipurpose Internet Mail Extensions (MIME)
- and more!

While some of these technologies have been in use for years, others, such as WSDL and UDDI, are very recent standards. But the greatest strength of the .NET Platform is perhaps that not only are these technologies in use but they are directly available to you to use. XML is probably the greatest example of this—not only does .NET communicate data internally and externally in XML but it lets you use the same plumbing to build your own custom solutions.

.NET was designed not only for building Internet solutions, but also for building Internet-enabled applications and services. Imagine traditional desktop or server applications that can dynamically, and without user involvement, connect to the Web as needed in a controlled and secure fashion. Although enabled solutions are possible, the architecture and development model and tools by no means dictate this; you can still build your traditional Windows style applications using the platform.

Addressing the Developer Challenges

The .NET Platform is designed not only to deliver more robust, feature laden solutions in new and improved ways but it addresses both the challenges that developers have long faced and those that confront end-user's, especially corporate customers. Chapter 2 highlighted some of the more demanding issues of pre-.NET development; this chapter will show how .NET addresses them.

Development

Three of the challenges pressing development are:

- Operating System centric development
- Restrictions and limitations of development language
- OS-centric and language-centric limitations of development tools

Perhaps you have heard reports that .NET is not tied to Windows—that it can run on different OSes. The fact is that at the time of printing, .NET is expected to be available only in the following Windows flavors: 95, 98, Me, NT, and 2000. However, the .NET framework is indeed platform agnostic by design. A good portion of the .NET framework library—an OS-independent subset—was submitted to ECMA on October 31, 2000 by Intel, Microsoft, and Hewlett-Packard for standardization. It is therefore possible that you will see one or more non-Windows versions in the near future.

Note

Actually, the submission included both the C# Programming Language (ECMA TC39/TG2) and the Common Language Infrastructure (ECMA TC39/TG3). If you are interested in the official submission visit, the ECMA Web site at http://www.ecma.ch or Microsoft's ECMA page at http://msdn.microsoft.com /net/ecma.

The few OS-dependent parts of the .NET architecture might need rewiring to make them run on some OSes but because these parts are isolated, the work required to move .NET to other platforms should prove minimal compared to the gain. Given Microsoft's staunch position that Windows is central to the future of computing coupled with the fact that Windows generates billions a year for Microsoft, it is astounding that they took such great pains to design .NET with platform-neutrality in mind.

Note

Third party companies are trying to port .NET to other platforms without Microsoft help. One such effort is driven by Southern Storm Software, Pty Ltd (http://www.southern-storm.com.au) with their Open.NET initiative.

In October 2000, Microsoft had not committed to making a version of .NET available on any other platform than Windows, although it had taken pains to make the platform portable. In a press release, however, Corel Software announced:

> "Microsoft has purchased 24 million non-voting convertible preferred shares at a purchase price of $5.625 (U.S.) per share or a total purchase price of $135 million (U.S.). The companies will also work together to support the development, testing, and marketing of new products related to the .NET platform. Joint-marketing initiatives will include participation in product launches and trade-show events and representation on mutual Web sites. In addition, both companies have agreed to settle certain legal issues between Corel and Microsoft."
>
> —Corel Corporation Press Release October 2000

In view of the fact that Corel competes with Microsoft not only in the productivity suite market but also in the operating system market, it was hard to fathom why Microsoft would invest in such a competitor if not for the reason of migrating .NET to other competing platforms (especially Linux) without doing the work directly.

Since then, Microsoft has announced that Corel Software will indeed work towards bringing .NET to at least one non-Windows operating system—namely FreeBSD Unix.

Microsoft certainly picked a strong partner when you consider the vast amount of Unix/Linux know-how Corel Corporation possesses. They not only have a Linux operating system offering but also have created Linux versions of their flagship products: CorelDraw and Corel WordPerfect. Couple this with the fact that in the late 1990s Corel created a Java version of WordPerfect that, although short lived, certainly gave the development team proficiency with creating large platform-agnostic, Internet-based applications. Certainly the Web and Web services aspects of .NET make delivering to any device possible but coupled with the possibility of running non-Web based applications on Linux makes "any device" take on even more meaning.

Note

For a great read on the birth of .NET and how it was a non-Windows initiative, read the October 30, 2000 cover story, "Microsoft's Big Bet," from *Business Week.*

As you learned in Chapter 2, development tools are more often than not bound to a specific OS, supported a limited number of programming languages (usually one) and come with a framework that is specific to the supported language and operating system.

Although languages themselves are not platform specific, they require tools (such as a compiler or interpreter) to transform them into an executable application and, unfortunately, more often than not these tools target one or a few specific operating systems. For instance, Microsoft Visual C++ compiles (transforms) programs written in the C or C++ language into running applications, but only for Microsoft Windows. It is not capable of targeting IBM AIX, MacOS, or any of the Linux flavors. The same follows for the *class libraries* (a.k.a. *frameworks*) that either come prepackaged with these tools or are available as add ons.

Sometimes you cannot even use class libraries across platforms. For example, frameworks targeted at a specific flavor of Unix, such as AIX, cannot run on another version of Unix, such as SCO or Solaris. The same can also hold for the different versions of Linux: RedHat, Corel, SuSe, and the like.

.NET shines in that the platform's framework, while written in C#, is designed with cross-platform and cross-language support in mind. As you will learn in Chapter 6, "Common Language Runtime," .NET defines rules that when adhered too make it possible for the platform to run programs not only written in one of many different languages but programs whose parts are written in different languages.

In the .NET world, however, the programming language is not specialized for a tool or operating system. Developers will be able to use one or more languages of their choosing, without having to interpret multiple dialects of the same languages. This means the developer can capitalize on existing programming language skills. If your company has invested heavily in Visual Basic, a Windows only language, it now becomes possible with .NET to create a solution that will run on a variety of devices. Perhaps you might even see Visual Basic applications running on Palm OS PDAs in the future!

In addition to the multi-language ability of the platform, you have cross-language compatibility. This does not just mean that developers can use their languages of choice but also that programs written in one language can call programs written in a different one.

Consider, for example, a project with 10 developers. Unfortunately, in this more than real scenario, the company does not have 10 available programmers with the same background—some have VB, a few C++, and others Java. In a non-.NET world you certainly can divide the team along development language skills, but this requires a lot of planning and effort. Part of this has to do with how objects are constructed, handled, and behave in different languages. Some of it has to do with the different interpretations of types. Part has to do with how methods are invoked and how memory is allocated and deallocated. Lastly, there is the issue of pointers, which exist in C++ but not in Java, for instance. This is where .NET shines! The common runtime and its components, which you'll learn more about soon, handle all these issues between languages seamlessly. Therefore, if the team writes its components in different languages and then ties them together, the pieces will fit as if they were written in the same language.

Now, *that* is powerful stuff. .NET provides native, seamless integration between data types, as well as use of objects and method calls across module or process boundaries. This is unique on such a broad scale. You cannot only find new ways to deliver current solutions but you can also create new ways to do so.

Delivery

.NET addresses the delivery challenges that face developers and corporations. Because .NET applications are not dependant on dynamic link libraries (DLLs) that are or may be shared between solutions, it avoids the DLL Hell common to Windows solutions today. .NET solutions are delivered as an "assembly" and do not have external dependencies in the same fragile and conflicting way as DLLs. Because they are nothing more than self-contained packages, this also means that you can install and run multiple versions of the same application without worry of conflict. For the developer this obviously means reduced testing and maintenance to address interactions with other software. For the corporate user this means that there is less of an issue when installing new .NET solutions.

Because the .NET platform makes developing, delivering and consuming Web services possible, which you will learn more about in the coming section, you can produce solutions whose feature list is as extensive as you like without the need to physically deliver all of them. Try to envision applications, such as Microsoft Office, that no longer ship with hundreds of megabytes of seldom-used features or features aimed at a niche market. Consider if these fat solutions came in slimmed down versions containing only a basic set of most commonly used functionality, whereas all the extra functionality is made available on demand, either free or at an additional cost. This concept of offering flexible, customizable solutions by leveraging the Web is a vision for software that Microsoft .NET delivers. This might even go as far as to deliver a CD version only to business customers, and only offering a downloadable subscription version to consumers.

Furthermore, delivering a smaller application with core features that are extended on demand will make electronic delivery more attractive to customers with low bandwidth Internet connections. It also makes it possible for you to more easily create one solution which targets different markets—the differentiation might be in what services come free at what price point, for example. From the end user side, this is also advantageous in that you can purchase or subscribe to a solution that meets your needs without the bulk and confusion of a "fully functional" solution packed with features you do not require.

Stability

Stability is one by-product of the assembly, as you learned. Another way that .NET facilitates more stable applications is the common language runtime. As you will learn more in Chapter 6, the runtime lets you forget about the memory issues such as access violations that often make producing stable software a challenge. The beneficial by-product of this is that it is not only easier to produce a more stable product but you get it in less time saving development costs. From a corporate perspective, increased stability is an obviously welcomed quality.

Security

As with stability, you will learn more about security in the Chapter 6, including the ability for developers to set system requirements within the software, which is a significant benefit. In .NET you can specify at code-level the operating system services your solution needs, such as hard disk access or Internet access. It is also possible to define what rights your solution grants other software that might make requests of it.

On the corporate side, an IT department is also able to set security policies for each assembly, tailoring security to corporate policies. You can, for example, designate that downloaded software from a certain company can access the local disk of a user but cannot do so with network disks or resources. These are just some of the stability and security benefits that managed execution brings to both developers and customers.

Maintenance

As you learned, .NET makes it possible for you to deploy different versions of the same solution. For developers, the versioning of assemblies makes it easier to support solutions—no question can arise as to whether a solution is using the correct version of a component it shipped with. From the end-user perspective, you gain the opportunity to test a new version while continuing to run your existing, tried-and-true solution.

On the other hand, by using Web services you can produce software updates that require no user intervention. The choice of manual or automatic maintenance is something that might depend on development organization and/or the corporate customer. .NET does not require automatic updates but simply facilitates them.

Introducing Web Services

Simply defined, Web services are software solutions delivered via the Web. They differ than traditional Web based solutions because they do not require an application interface and are designed to be integrated—or consumed—by other software solutions. This might be another Web service, a desktop application like Microsoft Word, a Web site or any other software "application" you might imagine. Web services are somewhat analogous to software components but they do not reside on the user's machine and are not (physically) contained within your solution. They are external service that your solution calls upon. A simple example of such a service might be a legal or dictionary that you ship with your word processing solution; useful but probably only to a small segment of your user base. From the end-user standpoint, solutions utilizing Web service might come packed with a cornucopia of features, most of which you might seldom use. As Web services, you do not need to install these features on your computer just in case you might require them in the future. Instead, they are made available to you only when you need them.

The business case for Web services is fairly strong and easy to imagine. It is perhaps easiest to think of .NET Web services in terms of cable television. Cable TV is a subscription model—it provides you with a choice of services (feature sets). With most cable providers, you can choose from at least two service tiers: basic cable, which provides only a core set of channels (basic features); and "basic plus" cable, which comes with a large number of channels. Then, as you know, there are the premium channels such as HBO, Disney, The Movie Channel, Cinemax, and others for which you pay an additional flat monthly subscription fee. Lastly, there are the pay-per-view channels that charge a varying per-program or per-day fee. The software of tomorrow might follow a very similar pricing and delivery plan, where the channels represent sets of features/services and the programs represent individual features. The major difference between pay-per-view programming and Web services will of course be that you don't have to wait until 8:00 EST for the "prime time" delivery of the service.

Web service enabled software is especially attractive in a corporate environment where different users in your company may require vastly different subsets of functionality. Your company needs only purchase and install the basic version of a solution—without crippling the power users. They could then gain access to the additional features on a per-use or some type of subscription basis using the Web as the delivery mechanism. Under a subscription scheme, the corporation can either subscribe directly on behalf of its user base or authorize or deny subscription rights to its users directly.

IBM, Sun Microsystems, and just about every other major company are jumping on the service bandwagon by creating their own infrastructure delivery solutions. The major advantage of .NET compared to some of the other platforms is that it delivers a more comprehensive set of standards based features and technologies. Among other things, .NET includes a single class framework library for building different types of solutions, makes it possible to use your preferred development language, is supported by a feature charged enterprise development tool and has infrastructure support from numerous enterprise class servers.

Microsoft formerly introduced one of the first and also most comprehensive Web service initiatives to date at its Professional Developer Conference (PDC) in October 2001: .NET My Services, formerly codenamed HailStorm.

.NET My Services

Microsoft has also announced that it will offer a slew of core services under the name of .NET My Services. .NET My Services is a collection of basic services aimed at giving users a more complete, seamless software experience. As powerful as Microsoft Outlook, Lotus Organizer, and other Personal Information Manager software are, these PIMs often lack the capability to easily and consistently share the data they manage and work with data generated by other solutions. Just consider trying to share your calendar with your favorite online travel agency. Consider personal digital assistants (PDAs), for example. If you are like millions of others using a PDA, you probably have felt the frustration of synchronizing your work or home PC with your PDA. Although software and hardware exists solely to facilitate synchronizing your data, it takes a conscious and concerted effort to actually do it—and sometimes the result isn't what you expect.

Having a repository for all your data that you can easily access from any application at any time with ease and efficiency would solve this problem.

Microsoft Passport takes a step toward solving this problem by providing one unified location to store your *personal* data. It falls short in that it currently is limited in functionality to user authentication and basic wallet functions. Furthermore, it does not adequately address the challenge of accessibility from *any* device.

User-Centric Services

.NET My Services is a user-centric collection of services aimed at giving you, the user, control of your data and empowering you to use that data to make your life easier.

.NET My Services are designed as services that are accessed by your application or Web portal. Before Microsoft codenamed these services as "HailStorm," they were known as building block services. This is because .NET My Services-are designed for inclusion in Microsoft and third-party solutions that then make these services available to you—they really are building blocks for developers.

For example, consider for a moment that you have a scheduling conflict with an appointment in Chicago. Using a .NET My Services-enabled application offering the .NET Calendar service, you can make that decision simply by going online, checking the .NET My Services-empowered travel Web site for the airline schedule, choosing the most convenient flight and letting the service cross-check your schedule for any conflicts. If none exist, the ticket could be seamlessly booked using your credit card, which is made available using the .NET Wallet service contained.

Meanwhile, a .NET My Services application can update your personal calendar with the flight details and e-mail a confirmation to your favorite mail account (as specified in your personal preferences). This scenario might certainly extend to booking a hotel and rental car based on certain pre-determined criteria.

These types of service solutions—Web services—are a large part of the .NET vision, and .NET My Services is an amalgamation of Web services that go a long way towards delivering the vision.

Note

.NET My Services are meant to be included by third-party solutions—be they Windows applications or Web solutions. As an end user you do not subscribe to Microsoft for the service but to your solution provider, who includes one or more of the services.

The Services of .NET My Services

.NET My Services will offer many of the personalized information management and organization features in the aforementioned example. The following are the initial service offerings[1]:

- .NET Alerts (Formerly myNotifications)—Provides subscription announcements/alerts, reports, management, and routing.
- .NET ApplicationSettings (Formerly codenamed myApplicationSettings)—Provides settings for applications.
- .NET Calendar (Formerly codenamed myCalendar)—Provides such time-management functions as setting tasks and scheduling appointments.
- .NET Categories—Provides the means to create personalized categories so that you can group information.
- .NET Contacts (Formerly codenamed myContacts)—Offers address and contact management, similar to an contacts in Outlook.
- .NET Documents (Formerly codenamed myDocuments)—Think: Universally accessible, secure hard drive for document storage.
- .NET Devices (Formerly codenamed myDevices)—Used to contain device settings and capabilities.
- .NET FavoriteWebSites (Formerly myFavoriteWebSites)—Provides a universally accessible way to store, retrieve and manage your favorite URLs and other Web identifiers. Your bookmarks will be available no matter which computer or device you are using.
- .NET Inbox (Formerly codenamed myInbox)—Similar to online mail today but offers more generic message management for e-mail, voice mail, faxes and more.
- .NET Lists—A service for creating general purpose lists. For example, a shopping list or a "to do" list.
- .NET Locations (Formerly codenamed myLocations)—Electronic and geographical location and rendezvous.
- .NET Presence—Online, offline, busy, free, which device(s) to send alerts to.
- .NET Profile (Formerly codenamed myProfile)—Name, nickname, special dates, picture, address.
- .NET Services (Formerly codenamed myServices)—Services provided for an identity.
- .NET Wallet (Formerly codenamed myWallet)—Receipts, payment instruments, coupons, and other transaction records.

For these services to work, it should be obvious that some kind of way to store and authenticate your identity is required. The basis of user authentication in

.NET My Services is Microsoft Passport. Microsoft's decision to use Passport as the entry point most likely is a tried and true Web service (even in its original incarnation, which was not based on open standards) that already has a large installed base of users.

Another reason one might imagine Microsoft chose Passport is that it is well known. Considering .NET My Services will face a degree of adoption resistance, like any new technology or product, using an widely known and accepted service as a springboard makes marketing sense. If you trust Passport to handle your on- and offline identity, as well as the personal information that facilitates shopping the Web, it is likely that you will also trust a Web address filing cabinet service from the same service provider.

The current previous incarnation of Passport maintained a personal information profile that included your name and address, and optionally account information for your credit card(s). These services make logging into Web sites a snap and shopping more convenient. While Passport retains its role as an authenticator, Microsoft has also broken out its subcomponents as individual services that you can integrate into your solutions: .NET Profile; .NET Location; .NET Wallet; and .NET Services.

Possible Effects of the .NET My Services

The services of .NET My Services provide basic building blocks for snapping together—more like tying together—user solutions centered on managing personal information and providing a user-centric experience. These services are aimed at e-commerce sites and other businesses with an on-line so that they can make their customer's experience more enriched. While .NET My Services appear more consumer oriented many of the services certainly can be used in a corporate environment. Also, given Microsoft's recent increase in enterprise-related development, it is only logical to expect them to eventually tailor .NET My Services to more specific business user requirements.

What can you expect from using .NET My Services and other Web services?

The idea of treating software as a service marks a significant departure from today's development models. On the one hand, Web services present an enormous opportunity for businesses because existing "know how" is locked up in isolated, system-centric solutions. Companies can still leverage Web services without giving away all their data. By making various aspects of their existing solutions Web-accessible, companies can make them available to their developers and users. For instance, your company or team might need to produce a new application that happens to have some feature overlap with an existing system. Given the resource and time costs involved in building software, why spend the time and money to redevelop a new solution when you have one that delivers some of the functionality you need?

Perhaps you have heard of the saying, "if it ain't broke, don't fix it." .NET not only makes building new Web services easy, it also facilitates exposing existing programs/parts of programs as Web services.

If you want to expose a Web service, say via the Internet, you must manually do so. So, by turning pieces of your applications into Web services you *can* then expose them for use, in a restricted way, to other solutions! If you are an IT manager involved in overseeing the migration of a Unix solution built in 1985 by the previously acquired company in the ungodly time frame of six months you may be drooling here, and with good reason! Certainly making your application accessible, either in part or in its entirety, is a means of migrating a solution. Chapter 10, "Migration Paths—From Anywhere to .NET," discusses migrating your solutions using.NET in more detail.

Obviously, the capability to turn existing code into Web services and then use them over the Internet or through the intranet to create new streams of revenue or simply as a means of reusing existing solutions will make a deep impact. One of the perhaps less obvious ways Web services will affect you, your development team, and your customers is the mental shift that has to take place. Creating software as a service is not fundamentally different but requires additional thought and consideration. Foremost is that services take components to a higher level. Most software components are self-contained and define certain functionality that they expose through APIs (or interfaces). These components are based on any given technology, say COM/COM+ for sake of argument, and as such "fit in" to a specific system or framework. In other words, they are building blocks but not universal ones.

Web services, on the other hand, are universally accessible, so nothing can be assumed about their use. They are isolated, result-oriented services that can be called from any operating system and whose results can be used in any fashion whatsoever. In a sense, they contradict with the rest of the object-oriented .NET platform in that consuming Web services is really function-oriented.

Summary

The .NET Platform delivers the promise and vision of building and using Web services. The software as services paradigm will change how many solutions are developed, delivered, maintained and purchased. As this is a new frontier for developers, end-users and businesses, there is now way to predict what the future will hold. Certainly you will see some flavors of the examples mentioned thus far, and surely many that are radically different. The enticing aspect of Web services is that it gives both producer and consumer a new, more flexible way to build and charge for solutions.

.NET is not "just" about Web services, however. As you now know, the .NET Platform addresses many of the challenges of traditional software development. It fixes the conflicts software have with each other due to the nature of Windows and DLLs; it liberates developers to use whatever language—or languages—they deem best for producing a solution; it addresses many security issues; and it delivers a versatile, enterprise class tool to produce .NET solutions with Visual Studio .NET.

4

What Is
.NET?

.NET is the amalgamation of the .NET Framework, the building block services known as .NET My Services (formerly known as HailStorm), which includes development tools such as Visual Studio.NET and infrastructure services provided by the .NET Enterprise Servers.

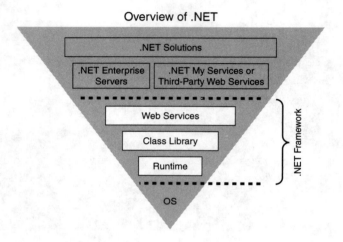

Figure 4.1

Overview of .NET highlighting the components of the .NET Framework.

At this juncture you should have a solid understanding of the vision of .NET and even possess some of the pieces that answer what it is. In the coming section of this book, you will begin to explore the .NET Framework. The material will, at times, venture into more technical detail than you have yet been exposed due to the simple fact that the material *is* technical. However, every effort is made to explain the technical details in as non-technical terms and manner as possible with the goal of making you see the advantages to .NET. During this descent into detail you will learn about the more important aspects of what makes .NET able to deliver on its promise. The goal is for you to grasp the advantages of .NET and the .NET Framework compared to the current development and delivery infrastructures.

Components of the .NET Framework

You already learned that the .NET Framework is a major component of .NET. Actually, it is *the foundation* and without it developers cannot construct .NET solutions. Although the Framework is itself composed of several components, unfortunately it seems that each white paper, news article, and book gives a slightly different definition of what those components are.

Some authors relegate the Framework to the building blocks, such as the classes—low-level program building blocks—used to build .NET solutions and the namespaces used to organize those classes, and view the common language runtime as a non-Framework core component. In contrast, most designate both the class libraries and runtime as part of the Framework, but differ on whether some or any services are part of the foundation. For example, there are diagrams that include "Web services" as a Framework component, whereas others designate ASP.NET as a component (presumably because current .NET Web services utilize ASP.NET). Even Microsoft's own documentation is at times inconsistent regarding this detail, as are many published articles.

The problem is one of subjectivity; without Microsoft clearly and consistently defining what Framework is for .NET, the debate will go on endlessly. The rationale behind making you aware that there is some literary inconsistency is to hopefully keep you from getting confounded should you continue your .NET education.

That said, the Framework *is* broken down into the following three parts:

- The common language runtime (CLR)
- The class libraries
- Services: both system (internal to .NET) and Web services

Together these components work in concert to make .NET what it is.

The classes and services are the parts that developers tie together to build solutions. Think of the common language runtime as the engine that runs the solutions. It sits between the operating system and your application and exposes your system services to you in a uniform, managed way.

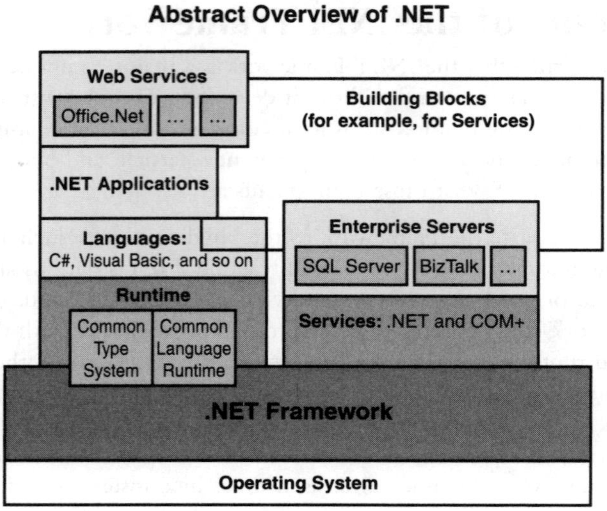

Abstract Overview of .NET

Figure 4.2

The common language runtime runs your solutions and makes your operating system services available.

Services of the Framework Components

The consistent opinion is that the Framework components work in concert to enable .NET solutions to run. These components deliver a wide assortment of services and functionality to the platform, including the following:

- Provides for input/output (I/O). I/O includes such operations as reading or writing a file, passing streams of data to and from somewhere, printing text to the screen or a printer, and so forth.
- Exposes Web technology and services including HTTP, HTML, XML, and SOAP.
- Provides user interface (UI) elements for building Web pages or traditional Windows forms–based interfaces.
- Facilitates building dynamic Web pages.
- Makes it possible to separate application logic and user interfaces when building dynamic Web pages using ASP.NET.
- Eases handling data from disparate data sources using ADO.NET.

- Ensures application and system security
- Utilizes runtime features such as garbage collection to improve application stability.
- Provides the means to build and deliver Web services.
- Makes it possible to leverage dozens of development languages including the new C#.
- Makes cross-language development and execution possible.
- Secures your investment in existing solutions, while providing a future-based development path.
- Offers a one-stop framework to build and deliver applications to any device.
- Makes new business opportunities viable by making new types of solutions possible.

Microsoft used the very same classes that are available to you in the Framework library to build .NET. From a development perspective, this *is* significant. It means developers have a great deal of functionality to build their solutions; after all, it doesn't get any better than building a solution for a platform using *the very same components used to build the platform* itself! This also aids you and your development team to understand the design principles underlying the platform from the .NET team's perspective and makes it more readily apparent how things *really* work, not just how the documentation says it is supposed to work. All these points aid you in building the best solutions you can and helps ensure that your solutions really work as intended—which certainly satisfies the user.

Before diving head first into the various aspects of the Framework, it's best to understand the two .NET facilitators: Visual Studio.NET and the .NET Enterprise Servers. These products are members of the .NET platform and, although they are not prerequisites to building or experiencing .NET solutions, they certainly augment it.

Visual Studio .NET

Visual Studio .NET is a .NET version of the ever-popular Microsoft Visual Studio. As you will learn later, in Chapter 8, "Visual Studio .NET," it offers an improved .NET integrated development environment (IDE) aimed at easing solution development on this evolutionary new platform. It contains project templates for creating just about every type of .NET-oriented solution you can imagine, including Windows forms-based applications, which are your traditional (Microsoft Windows) UI-based applications; Web Services; ASP.NET applications; database-driven solutions; and enterprise-level solutions.

The tool improves on its predecessor's concept of visual programming, combining the power of Microsoft Visual C++ with the ease of the Visual Basic 6.0 forms programming model and development environment. For instance, developers can design much of the application using a drag-and-drop paradigm familiar to Visual Basic. A toolbox contains all the control elements available for the type of project you are working with. For example, for creating a Windows forms application, which is the .NET name for a traditional Windows style program, the toolbox contains data elements, user interface (Windows Forms) controls, and some generally useful components.

The database support and wizards help you connect your solution to a data store are also aimed squarely at making development more efficient. Furthermore, if you are a Visual Studio 6 user, you will find the added support for HTML, XML, XMLSchema, and the third-party XSLT support a God-send! Visual Studio .NET also builds on the type-safe programming concept underlying the .NET libraries and offers statement completion and both pre-compile and compile-time checking. It also features a new help feature, called "dynamic help" that actively brings up help topics associated to the current context of your code and the features of the tool you are currently working with.

Note

Because Visual Studio .NET supports third-party plug-in modules, expect a market of useful productivity tools that seamlessly integrate into it.

.NET Enterprise Servers

As you will learn in Chapter 9, "An Introduction to the .NET Enterprise Servers," unlike the marketing name suggests, the nine .NET Enterprise Servers are neither built atop the .NET platform nor are they a required component of the platform. As it turns out, the servers were far ahead of .NET in the development cycle to be native .NET servers—there's no .NET in them. SQL Server 2000, BizTalk Server 2000, and Exchange Server 2000 were all shipping products long before .NET even entered the Beta 2 testing cycle. Regardless, these servers provide added infrastructure value for building and running .NET solutions.

For instance, SQL Server 2000 speaks the extensible markup language (XML) and integrates well with both BizTalk Server 2000 and ADO.NET, which is the data-centric component of .NET for working with data from any data source (for example, your database). ADO.NET is the successor to ActiveX Data Objects (ADO), which is a standard means of working with data in Windows today. Besides the fact that it talks XML, it provides methods for handling data that are optimized for SQL Server 2000.

BizTalk server, the messaging, integration, and workflow server, is probably the most .NET server of the nine enterprise servers. The first "all new" Microsoft server product in some time, BizTalk Server 2000 builds walking bridges across the chasms that lie between today's enterprise applications. Most notably, it makes connecting solutions that talk in complex electronic document interchange (EDI) formats with applications that exchange data using other formats, such as the SWIFT format or XMLSchema. Because of its strong XML roots and its function as an integrator of messages, BizTalk Server compliments the .NET platform when it comes to building or extending enterprise applications using .NET.

As you might imagine, each of these servers brings to the .NET platform its own strengths that help developers and IT personnel create robust, feature rich solutions. You will learn more about the servers later in this book.

- SQL Server 2000
- BizTalk Server 2000
- Exchange Server 2000
- Host Integration Server 2000
- Internet Security and Acceleration Server 2000
- Application Center 2000
- Commerce Server 2000
- Mobile Information 2001 Server
- SharePoint Portal Server 2001

Summary

The Framework and the .NET Enterprise Servers deliver the infrastructure which you can easily leverage with Visual Studio .NET to assemble solutions ranging from the desktop to the enterprise. The coming chapters will expand on each of these aspects of .NET, giving you a better idea of the features and power the platform brings you.

ORCHESTRATION • SECURITY • NAM
VISUAL STUDIO .NET • JUST-IN-TIME
GARBAGE COLLECTOR • LANGUAGE
DENCE • COMMON LANGUAGE RUI
SERVICES • CLASS LIBRARY • .NET FF
ENTERPRISE SERVERS • MIGRATION •
ORCHESTRATION • SECURITY • NAM
VISUAL STUDIO .NET • JUST-IN-TIME
GARBAGE COLLECTOR • LANGUAGE
DENCE • COMMON LANGUAGE RUI
SERVICES • CLASS LIBRARY • .NET FF
ENTERPRISE SERVERS • MIGRATION •
ORCHESTRATION • SECURITY • NAM
VISUAL STUDIO .NET • JUST-IN-TIME
GARBAGE COLLECTOR • LANGUAGE
DENCE • COMMON LANGUAGE RUI

Dissecting the .NET Framework

5

Introducing the Class Library

Perhaps you are familiar with object-oriented programming languages or systems. The basic concept is that everything is broken down or defined in terms of self-contained components, known as *objects*. The goal behind such design is to encapsulate the data pertaining to the object and define the means to both access and manipulate the object. In other words, the object knows about itself and can therefore manage itself. For example, a window "knows" how to be opened, closed, locked, and unlocked and it has well defined operations that you can perform to change its state, from closed to open, for instance.

Using the object paradigm to design and implement software is more intuitive and the result has benefits over the procedural-based alternatives. Using a procedural language, such as C or Pascal, requires less "start up" time during analysis and design and *can* take less time to implement than an object-oriented solution. However, proper object-oriented design yields a blue print from which developers have objects whose functionality is well defined and isolated from the rest of the system. This makes it easier to distribute the development tasks to a team. Because the system's design was "objectified" from the beginning, the interfaces between objects are well defined. This means that once each member is finished producing his or her components, the resulting objects can be "snapped" together. This isolation of functionality means that the objects can be reused in another solution and makes the solution more manageable—for example when it comes to updating the solution or performing maintenance. As an analogy, once a glass window is created for the current colonial house, it can later be reused in a Tudor-style home; that's a power of objects.

Several languages have emerged from the object-oriented philosophy including Smalltalk, Object Pascal, C++, and Java. Although some of these languages come "bundled" with a framework or system, such as Java's Abstract Windows Toolkit (AWT), most are simply languages with grammar aimed at making the expression of objects easier—they facilitate writing object-oriented programs. For example C++ defines the class keyword to facilitate declaring and defining objects. As you might expect, the emergence of any new programming language is soon followed by the introduction of tools and frameworks.

For example the introduction of C++ by Bjarne Stroustrup was soon followed by Borland's Borland C++ development suite, which included both a C++ *compiler* and a C++ framework called the Object Windows Library (or OWL for short), and Microsoft Visual C++, which introduced the Microsoft Foundation Classes (MFC). Both OWL and MFC are frameworks that make developing Windows applications in C++ easier.

The .NET Platform and Framework followed in a similar evolutionary path in that Microsoft defined a new language, C# (pronounced C-sharp), and introduces with it the .NET Platform. Although the platform is a system not a language or framework, its creation would not have been possible in its current manifestation without the development of the C# language and the .NET Framework. C# was used to write the .NET Framework, which in turn was used to write the platform itself.

Note

A few words regarding C#. This language is a close relative of C++ and, like its predecessor, it is an object-oriented language. You will learn in the coming sections that it takes many of the object concepts of C++ and other familial languages one step further. In acknowledgment to its heritage, many of the C# constructs and keywords are borrowed from C++. Syntactically and structurally, a C++ programmer will easily understand C# at first glance. The differences between the two languages are mostly small refinements and the more significant differences lean toward making C# an easier language to learn and use "out of the box." The ease at which a transition from C++ (or even Java) to C# is accomplished is important to mention because undoubtedly the initial reaction of many existing C++ or Java developers—not to mention their managers—will be one of trepidation. New languages certainly present challenges to development teams; however should you or your developers decide to switch to C#, rather than use one of the other .NET compliant languages, the transition will prove surprisingly painless.

As you will learn, one aspect that sets .NET apart from some of the other members of the object-oriented camp is that .NET is not just oriented towards objects—*everything* in the .NET Framework is an object, *including* simple and built-in data types. This object consistency makes working with the library more intuitive and contributes to .NET's clean design and implementation. It also promotes stability because there is less complexity—everything is an object, period.

Overview of Types

At the core, programming is the science (and sometimes the art) of working with data. Information is stored, modeled, and massaged—manipulated—in countless ways. The end goal provides the guidelines for the type of data required, imbues it with semantics, and defines how to manipulate it. Obviously, to begin with,there must be some way to represent, store, and work with data, for which programming languages (and frameworks) provide various *data types*.

Built-In Types

The following discussion refers to the sample user registration Web page shown in Figure 5.1.

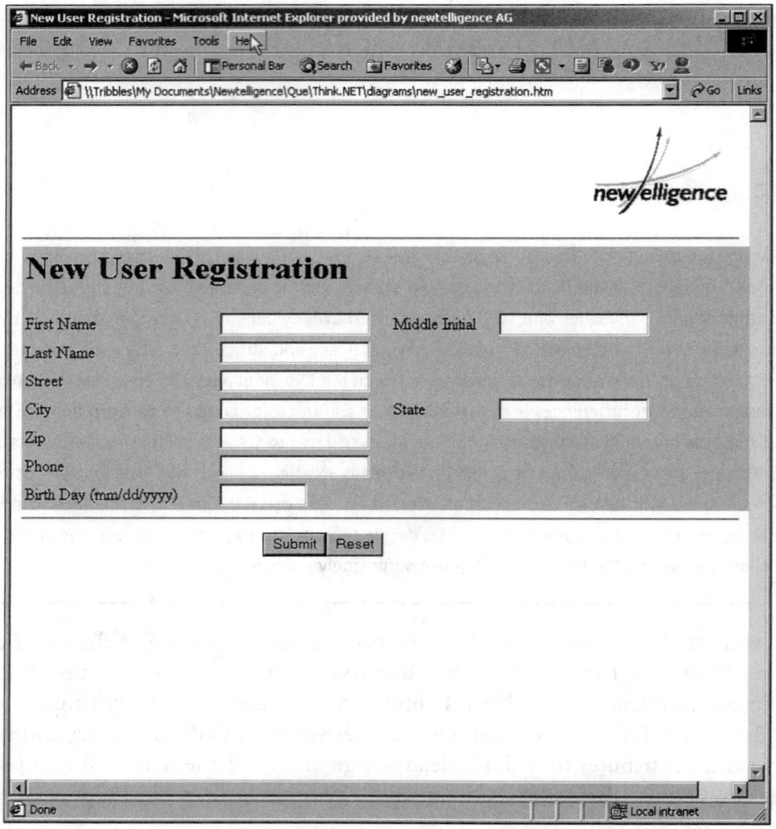

Figure 5.1

A user registration Web page.

The page is comprised of several edit boxes for you to enter your personal information. For the the first name, last name, street, and city fields, the data entry can be composed of alphanumeric characters (A/a–Z/z), as well as numbers and special characters, such as hyphens and accents.

Behind every one of the edit boxes, a means of storing the information is required, so that the program has a chance to do "something" with it. The container must be compatible with the data you enter and needs to not only store it but also to provide the means to manipulate it later. These data containers are actually instances—or variables—of data types. In the previous example, the .NET data type that best fits your needs is the String type.

Programming languages have a set of data built-types that are intrinsic to the language. For example, the following are some of the intrinsic C++ types: `int` (for integers); `float` (for decimal numbers); `char` (for representing a single character); `double` (for longer—double length—decimal numbers); and `byte`. Unlike user- or framework-defined types, the underlying construction of intrinsic type is hidden from view. For example, C++ does not have a built-in string type, but the C++ library provides a `string` class that you can use as if it were a built-in type.

Table 5.1 lists the built-in types that the .NET Framework library contains for working with the most common types of information.

Table 5.1 Framework Type Descriptions

Framework Library Types (found in the `System` Namespace)	Description
Boolean	True/false value.
Char	A 16-bit Unicode character.
Object	Object or boxed value type; the base for all types, classes, and so on in the framework library.
String	Used to represent an immutable text string. Uses the Unicode character set.
Single	IEEE 32-bit floating number. A single precision 32-bit value ranging from $-3.40282346638528859e38$ to $+3.40282346638528859e38$.
Double	IEEE 64-bit float. Used to represent double precision 64-bit decimal values ranging from $-1.79769313486231570e308$ to $+1.79769313486231570e308$.
Sbyte	Signed 8-bit integer. Can represent an integer from −128 through +127.
Int16	Signed 16-bit integer. Can represent an integer from −32768 through +32767.
Int32	Signed 32-bit integer. Can represent an integer from −2,147,483,648 through +2,147,483,647.
Int64	Signed 64-bit integer. Can represent an integer from −9,223,372,036,854,775,808 through +9,223,372,036,854,775,807.
IntPtr	Signed integer, native size.
TypedReference	Pointer plus runtime type.
Byte	Unsigned 8-bit integer.
UInt16	Unsigned 16-bit integer. Can represent an integer from 0 through 65535.

Table 5.1 Framework Type Descriptions Continued

Framework Library Types (found in the System Namespace)	Description
UInt32	Unsigned 32-bit integer. Can represent an integer from 0 through 4,294,967,295.
UInt64	Unsigned 64-bit integer. Can represent an integer from 0 through 184,467,440,737,095,551,615.
Decimal	Can represent positive and negative *values* with 28 significant digits, ranging from +79,228,162,514,264,337,593,543,950,335 through −79,228,162,514,264,337,593,543,950,335. Designed for currencies, financial calculations, or when any large number of significant digits and no round-off errors are required.

A Fully Object-Oriented Framework

As mentioned, in contrast to most object-oriented systems, all data types in .NET are objects; recall that *everything* in the framework, even primitive types, is derived from (are descendants of) one granddaddy of them all: System.Object. Although you might think of data types in the current context as "simple types" (decimal, character, and so on), classes themselves can define types. In the .NET Framework, even the simplest data type exposes properties and methods by which to manipulate them.

Note

System.Object is actually the qualified name of the class Object. System is the namespace to which Object belongs. You will learn more about namespaces in the "Framework Organization: Namespaces" section.

For example, the String object type has a length property that returns the length of the string and a char property for returning the character located at a specified position in the string. It also contains a slew of additional useful methods including:

- `Equals`: Determines whether two character strings are equal.

- `Substring`: Returns a substring of the string contained by the `String` object.

- `StartsWith`: Determines whether the character string starts with a specified character or string of characters.

- `ToUpper`: Returns the string, converted to all uppercase characters.

- `ToInt32`: Converts the character string to an integer of type `Int32`—a .NET data type for 32-bit integers.

Note

In principle, `string` is a simple value type, but technically it is a reference type and is only used here to illustrate the point.

By making `System.Object` the foundation (or base) of everything in the library, .NET is fully object oriented. Among the benefits of this is that it provides a consistent way to handle objects. Additionally, certain behavior and operations are inherent to all objects. For example, all classes inherit the following methods from `System.Object`: Equals; GetHashCode; GetType; ReferenceEquals; and ToString. Each object descendant is then free to override these methods with specialized context or meaning.

The `Equals`, `ReferenceEquals`, `GetType` and `ToString` methods are particularly interesting. The two equality methods are of particular interest because object equality can have two connotations: *value* and *reference*.

If you create two `Customer` objects, for example, and initialize them with the same data, they are considered separate instances of the same `Customer`. However, because they have the same value, they are "value equal."

```
// Create two Customer object instances
Customer A = new Customer();
Customer B = new Customer();
    // Initialize Customer object A and B with different data
A.SetData("Samantha Hollings");
B.SetData("Samantha Hollings");
    // We now have 2 Customer objects A & B that are value equal
```

Given `Customer` objects A and B, if you were to change the values of `Customer` B to differ in some way from A, the objects would no longer be value equal.

```
    // Set Customer object A and B with different data
A.SetData("Samantha Hollings");
B.SetData("Bill Clinton");
    // We now have 2 Customer objects A & B that have unequal values
```

The second notion of equality is reference equality. This has to with the capability to create two objects, for example, Customer objects A and B, and have them both refer to the same instance. This is different than value equality because now there are not two distinct object instances that simply have the same value, there is one object instance that both objects reference. Assigning one object to the other as in the following example does this:

```
B = A;
```

The capability to perform both types of equality checks on any objects in the library is important. For this reason, default implementations are built into System.Object. However, because the system cannot know what it means to be equal outside of two objects referencing the same instance, the default implementation of the Equals method only provides for checking reference equality. If you require value equality comparison, you must override the Equals operator and provide your own code to evaluate such conditionals. The ReferenceEquals method, on the other hand, is meant to report when two objects reference the same instance.

Following is defines the other member methods of the Object class:

- Finalize is called when the object is to be garbage collected. Interestingly, though, by default it does nothing, as it is meant to be overridden by a subclass. Note that although Finalize is not called until the object is reclaimed, there is no guarantee that it will actually be called or at what point.
- GetType method discovers the type of an object. This is often useful (if not necessary) at runtime to determine whether one object is of the same *type* as another.
- MemberwiseClone is called to create an exact copy of the object.
- ToString returns a string representation of the object instance.

The ability to inherit functionality and properties from one object to another, and to then to tailor the behavior is a powerful feature of object-oriented languages and systems—and a necessity. You will learn more about the concept in the section about inheritance.

Understanding Classes

Classes are the way that you declare and define your own objects in .NET. Objects in .NET—or any object-oriented system—have properties and methods that, combined, describe the object and provide the means to work with the object. Properties contain state information and values that describe the object. In the case of an object that represents a geometric object, the properties might include height, width, length. The methods expose the means to alter the properties and perform operations on the object. For example, there might be a scale method to increase or decrease a geometric objects size.

By building a solution using objects, the parts of the solution tend to be more logically and functionally isolated in a way that makes building, managing and updating them easier. An additional benefit is that in an object-oriented system like the .NET Framework, you can use existing objects as the basis for new ones.

Note

The use of an object is accomplished by instantiating it, which you can think of as copying it from a template. If you use Microsoft Word, you can think of a class definition as a document template. When you create a new document based on a template, you are creating an instance (instantiating an object) of that document template (class).

You either use prefabricated classes, such as the string class, or build new ones. You might create a new class from the ground up or build one by deriving it from an existing one.

Class by Example

Like Borland's OWL or Microsoft's MFC, the .NET Framework provides an assortment of user interface classes to simplify building solution facades. Each of the UI components is specialized, offering a different purpose, behavior, and look. Some are designed for containing, manipulating, and presenting lists of data, whereas others are meant for singular data items.

Consider the TextBox control as a concrete example of a .NET interface class. Visually, the service this element provides is the ability to display data in a box on the screen. Operationally, it permits keyboard input and provides methods to change the text box's behavior or appearance.

Similar to objects in the real world, classes can have *properties* that in combination help describe the object's state of existence, physical appearance (in the case of UI elements), and behavior.

For example, the TextBox control has a BackColor property that defines the background color of the edit box and a BorderStyle property that determines the style of the box's border. Additionally it has behavioral properties, such as CharacterCasing—which determines whether the control automatically sets the casing of entered text—and MaxLength—which sets the maximum number of characters the user can type into the box.

Unlike real-world objects whose properties are generally defined at "fabrication," properties of a class are used to either set an attribute of the object or to retrieve it. The difference depends on whether the property is used or an assignment is made to it.

For instance, `TextBox.BackColor` retrieves the background color of the control, whereas `TextBox.BackColor = Blue` sets the background color to blue.

Unlike construction materials, classes have *methods*, which can alter object properties or provide a restricted means of using the object. Looking back to the `TextBox`, this class has methods to alter the properties and manipulate the element in different ways, such as setting the text string displayed, retrieving the characters the user types, and rescaling its size. For example, using the `Scale` method, you can resize the control to 150% of its current size: `TextBox.Scale(150)`.

Functionality Through Framework Classes

The .NET Framework offers a variety of classes aimed at providing you with a rich set of predefined functionality and behavior. The classes in the framework compose what in computer lingo is called a *library*. The difference between a real-world one and the framework library is that, instead of containing thousands of books covering different topics of interest, the framework library is composed of thousands of classes organized by what are known as namespaces. These classes provide a plethora of functionality for just about anything a developer needs, including classes that:

- Expose "system" functionality, such as the means to access, create, and manipulate files.
- Offer mathematical functionality including trigonometric functions.
- Provide containment for organizing and working with collections of data objects.
- Provide the underlying security structures for the .NET system.
- Offer countless user interfaces controls.
- Make it easier to create or work with XML documents.
- Expose the complete HTTP infrastructure.
- Simplify existing COM/COM+ based components or applications from within .NET solutions.
- Provide the plumbing used by the common language runtime, such as garbage collection, threading, process management, and security.

It might help to think of the .NET Framework as both a carpenter's toolbox and a lumber supply company combined. It is choc-full of tools and materials with which developers build solutions.

Rest assured, .NET comes with the power, flexibility, and ease of use to create best-of-breed solutions. Whether or not you are a developer if you take a look at the *.NET Framework Reference* its hierarchical, straightforward, common sense design will surprise you. Microsoft has obviously put a great deal of thought and effort into designing and building the .NET Framework—and it shows!

Framework Organization: Namespaces

Speaking in general programming terms, a namespace is a way to logically or semantically group similar declarations or definitions together in a way that makes them uniquely identifiable. It is essentially a way to create packages of functionality that can be included or referenced from different parts of a program. In this way, namespaces facilitate better organization of classes. Because namespaces package function logically, they facilitate use, make development more manageable, and let you include only the functionality you need in your solution. If your task is to create the back-end processing part of a product ordering system, you don't want to needlessly beef up your solution with user-interface functionality. In a similar vein, you probably want to include the classes that facilitate working with data and storing it to the company database. Using namespaces, finding and using such targeted functionality is simplified.

Namespace organization is done using a "dot syntax" notation, which aids in making each namespace globally unique. If you consider the framework library as a library of classes, the namespace corresponds to the Dewey decimal system or Library of Congress classification for cataloging and arranging books.

The namespace hierarchy is from left to right, with the leftmost name as the root. For example, the `System.Web` namespace contains the classes that make browser/server (Web) communication possible. Making classes from a namespace available to your program simply requires that you include the namespace. You do this by declaring its use in each file that requires access to the namespace. For example, the following declares that you will use the System.Web namespace:

```
using System.Web;
```

Once the namespace is included its classes can be used without qualification. For example, in the following code snippet a `HttpCookie` is declared, called `myCookie`, and an instance is instantiated (that's the `= new …` part). This creates a Web browser cookie, named `myVeryOwnCookie`.

```
HttpCookie myCookie = new HttpCookie( "myVeryOwnCookie");
```

However, it is possible to omit the `using` declaration, in which case, full qualification of the class is required whenever it is used:

```
System.Web.HttpCookie myCookie = new System.Web.HttpCookie(
➥"myVeryOwnCookie");
```

The use of the dot-syntax naming convention of namespaces in .NET combined with the names and organization the .NET team selected makes for a library that is amazingly easy to navigate and comprehend. Even if you aren't a programmer, you can surmise a great deal of the functionality available, understand how things are put together, and determine where to find what you need should you decide to program in .NET. Figure 5.2 takes a deeper look at the System.Web namespace hierarchy.

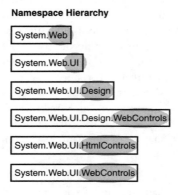

Namespace Hierarchy

System.Web

System.Web.UI

System.Web.UI.Design

System.Web.UI.Design.WebControls

System.Web.UI.HtmlControls

System.Web.UI.WebControls

Figure 5.2

Example of the namespace hierarchy and how namespaces extend one another.

Presumably, you can surmise some of what the different Web namespaces do, even without examining the classes they contain. For instance, System.Web.UI.WebControls contains user interface (UI) classes for creating the visuals of a Web page, including but not limited to the Button, CheckBox, DataList, (text) Label and TextBox controls. Likewise, you can conclude that System.Web.Services and its sub-namespaces (Description, Discovery, Protocols) contain classes that enable you to create Web Services—which they do.

In addition to logically grouping classes in easily decipherable, unified libraries, namespaces are extensible. You can derive your own namespaces from existing ones in the same way that classes can serve as bases to other classes through derivation. For example, if you find that the Web controls contained by System.Web.UI do not meet your needs, you can create your own custom UI elements and package them into your own namespace. To create your own namespace you simply declare and create a scope for your namespace with {and} as follows:

```
namespace System.Web.UI.YourCompany
{
    //...
}
```

Everything between the brackets is then part of your newly created namespace.

Note

In case you are wondering what the System namespace is, the name implies it all; it contains the fundamental classes defining the data types and other functionality common to the rest of the framework—the "system" services needed to build and run your solutions.

One last point about namespaces is that Microsoft has published some naming guidelines that are highly recommended to provide naming consistency, prevent confusion, and help avoid naming "collisions" between namespaces from different development organizations.

The general rule when creating namespaces is to use *CompanyName.TechnologyName*, such as YourCompany.Web. Additionally, it makes sense to use similar casing techniques as Microsoft, which is to capitalize the first character in each word and not to use hyphenation (this is also known as Pascal casing). For example, use YourCompany.WebServices rather than YourCompany.Web-Services or YourCompany.Webservices. Lastly, to avoid confusion, it is not a good idea to name a class with the same name as a namespace. For instance, do not create a WebServices class when a namespace with the same name exists.

Single Inheritance

You learned a little bit about inheritance when you read the about System.Object and how all things spring up from this defining class.

Note

You learned earlier that everything in .NET is an object. You can actually declare a new class and not inherit from an existing library class but it is still an object. How? Inheritance from System.Object is actually implicitly.

.NET classes provide you almost everything you need to build the infrastructure of your solution, but at some point you are likely to find a particular class that does almost what you need, but not quite. As you already read, you can use the existing classes as the foundation upon which to build new classes that you tailor to your needs. The process of deriving one class from another is called *inheritance*.

The result of inheritance is a bit like giving birth to a new child. You create a new class by declaring it as a descendant of an existing class (in computer parlance: derive from an existing class). Like genetics, it means the new class gets "all" the stuff of its parents but—luckily perhaps—it does not mean it is exactly the same. What happens is that your new (child) class inherits the properties, methods, interfaces, and behavior of its parent (formerly called a "base class"), but you are then free to develop it into a similar but distinctly different entity. The specialization takes several forms. First the existing inherited properties, methods, and behaviors can be overridden—that is from the outside they are the same but internally they are altered—or additional properties and methods can be added.

Figure 5.3 is a diagrammatic example of deriving two specialized text boxes from a common base class, TextBox. Although both of the new classes, TextBoxFancy and TextBoxPassword, inherit the Text and Enabled properties from the base class, they require further specialization; their names clearly indicate that they have different purposes. If you examine the new properties of TextBoxPassword you can see that there is a minimum length for text (MinLength) and a property for setting that the text is masked (MaskText), as all passwords should be. The TextBoxFancy, in contrast, adds the ability to set the foreground and background colors.

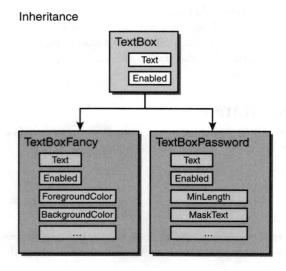

Figure 5.3

Example of single inheritance from a TextBox class.

Multiple Inheritance

The .NET Platform does not support the ability to take two objects and inherit from them simultaneously to create a new hybrid object. If you have a C++ background, you might be one of the few developers that will scream in anguish to learn that .NET does *not* support multiple inheritance.

It can certainly be useful to inherit from two objects simultaneously, also known as *multiple inheritance*. For example, you might have two user-interface controls that have properties and methods that, combined, have what you need in a new element.

For this reason, some developers might consider this loss of expression and functionality unacceptable. However, the fact is that multiple inheritance is seldom used because it is one of those things that is great conceptually but a nightmare in practice. The power is not worth the headache of getting it to work (and only the best developers can get it to work properly in the real world). More to the point, knowing that only single inheritance is permissible, good software architects can achieve the same robustness of design and implement the solution quicker and more reliably.

In C++ for example, deriving two classes B and C from class A is straightforward and any functionality defined in A is inherited by B and C; as you know, this is single inheritance.

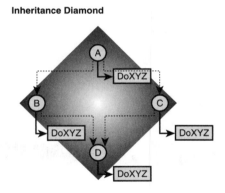

Inheritance Diamond

Figure 5.4

Multiple inheritance: The inheritance diamond.

Now, assume that a class D is the logical descendent of B and C—it is a combination of the two objects. With multiple inheritance you can derive D from both B and C and gain access to the features of both. In the C++ language, declaring such an object is easy; it is implementing it properly that is the challenge.

For example, you know that B and C implement DoXYZ. Now, because D inherits from both classes, it inherits two identical-looking methods. Assuming D does not override DoXYZ because its B implementation is sufficient, a problem arises. Although you might want and expect B's implementation to be used when you call DoXYZ from D, how does it know to use B's and not C's implementation? This is the problem programmers must address and is exactly the type of "feature" that introduces unintended program behavior. It might prove easy enough to handle in this scenario when the object hierarchy is composed of only four classes, but once it becomes deeper it becomes more difficult to manage. Even more challenging is when you are using a library built with multiple inheritance and the behavior you expect is not what you get—for example, you use the D object thinking that it executes B's DoXYZ when in reality it executes C's. Figure 5.5 will give you a clearer idea of the issue.

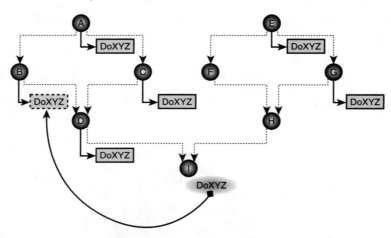

Figure 5.5

Resolving methods when using multiple inheritance.

Creating Interfaces

Interfaces provide a means for software developers to support functionality, which they do not necessarily write themselves.

Interfaces can be viewed from two perspectives. First, they comprise a declaration of services that are declared but not fulfilled (they are not implemented). Essentially, they are service contracts that are written but not signed, so no one is required to accept these contracts and no one is obligated to fulfill them. Each contract is simply proposed for adoption but they are not mandatory. If a software component (such as a class) decides to accept a proposed service, that class must, in a manner of speaking, "sign" the contract and then becomes bound to implement the service. Inheriting the interface does the "signing" of the contract.

Note

In the inheritance section, you learned that multiple inheritance is not permitted in .NET. This is not exactly true—multiple *implementation* inheritance is not permitted (inheriting from multiple classes); multiple interface inheritance is permitted. This has to do with the fact that implementation of any inherited interface must be done by the class inheriting the interface(s), so there can be no confusion as to which implementation the class should use during program execution.

Interface by Example

Interfaces can help your development team by permitting the definition of various service-level contracts that components in the system can then agree to implement as needed. For example, most companies have customers and they most certainly have addresses.

Using the power of interfaces, you can then declare interfaces for such services as outputting or inputting the customer name or address. You or another developer can then choose to inherit one or more interfaces that make sense to provide for the actual "customer information" component. In this way, the `Customer` class can implement various interfaces for handling such information as a customer's name, address, company name, telephone number, and the like. The `Customer` component can be designed to inherit from an `IFormatAddress` interface, which defines an output-only service for formatting the address. By doing so, the `Customer` class does not inherit any already defined implementation but only publishes a contract to do so. In this way, several classes can offer the same generic interface and implement the interface in the manner specific to their needs.

Assume for example that the `IFormatAddress` interface promises to provide a way to get and set an address. The type of address, the local format, or even the layout of the address is not provided. Assume your solution needs to handle the `Customer` and the `SalesPerson` associated with each customer. Both have addresses but they can differ in various respects. By inheriting the `IFormatAddress`, both publicly promise to fulfill the means of setting and retrieving the `Customer` and `SalesPerson` objects' addresses.

In .NET declaration of an interface is done using the interface keyword, whereas implementation is handled by inheriting one or more interfaces when declaring/defining a class.

One great benefit of declaring a contract of services this way is that it guarantees backward compatibility for the consumers of the software. Because the interface does not have any implementation details, future versions will not break the contract. If a producer wants to offer a "new and improved" service contract, it can simply declare a new interface that the consumer is free to implement or ignore—without penalty.

Using Containers/Collections

Another basic but important set of classes provided for you in the framework are the collection classes. Collections are a set of specialized classes designed to make working with related data easier by not only providing a way to group the data but by providing the means to manipulate it. The assortment of available classes covers the basic types of collections found in computer science, from arrays to hash tables. There are several collection classes available to you or your developers to use and from which to build your own more specialized collection.

The collection types include Array, ArrayList, ObjectList, Queue, Stack, SortedList, Hashtable (note the lack of camel casing is an exception here), and DictionaryEntry. As you might expect, each of these provides the means to add, remove, and modify members of a collection and some, such as the SortedList class, offer methods to sort contained items (see Figure 5.6).

Note

The fact that all components of the framework are derived from System.Object makes universal collections possible. The collections do not need to know which type of object they are working with but instead simply work with the base class. In object-oriented programming this is called *polymorphism*. Without this ability, you would need a different type of collection for each type of item it should work with.

The benefit of providing classes for such common tasks as implementing a queue certainly makes development easier and quicker. Not only do you not need to write your own classes for these common tasks, but you do not need to quality assure them—the Microsoft development team has handled both for you already.

Collections

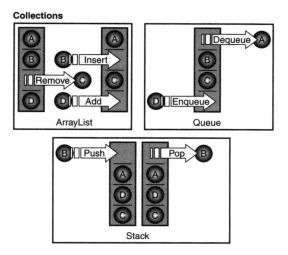

Figure 5.6

The `ArrayList`, `Stack`, and `Queu` collections and their "add" and "remove" operations.

ADO.NET

While collections provide you with the most basic means of working with logically related data, they are little help for more complex sets of data or relational data. To this end, the .NET Framework class library includes additional classes that fall under the designation of ADO.NET.

Some Difference to ADO

ADO.NET is the successor to ActiveX Data Objects (ADO) that is commonly used by Visual Basic 6 and Visual C++ developers to work with data from a database. The similarities between the two technologies, however, stop at that point. Unlike ADO, ADO.NET has no ActiveX in it—in other words it is not COM/COM+ based. Furthermore, while ADO was originally designed to work with data directly on a database, ADO.NET is designed to work with data in a more general manner. That is, it lends itself well to use even without a database. For example, if your application needs to record and store on the local computer user and application preferences there is no need to require a database for this. ADO.NET can easily be used without a database, reading and writing to and from files for instance. Furthermore, because it uses XML to represent data internally, it is also able to read and write XML data making it ideal for Web based applications.

A significant between ADO.NET and ADO is that the former was designed from the ground up with the Web in mind. The use of XML is obviously one feature towards this. The second is that it uses a disconnected data model, which means that a fixed connection to a database is neither required nor permit. By design, ADO.NET promotes the same "hit-and-run" model as the Web: connect (to the database), retrieve the data, disconnect (from the database), manipulate the data, reconnect (to the database) and update any changes.

An additional advantage to ADO.NET is that it is data-oriented, not record oriented. The main data storage and manipulation class is the *DataSet* (found in *System.Data*). This class does not directly contain the data (as a *RecordSet* in ADO does) but contains a collection of *DataTable* objects each of which is used to hold logically related data information, such as "customers". Because the *DataSet* can have more than one *DataTable*, data is stuffed into one and only one table as with ADO. This gives you the opportunity to model and work with your data relationally in the same way that modern relational databases do.

Note

You can think of ADO.NET as your universal data access and manipulator—it is not just for working with databases but *any* data source.

The flexibility of the *DataSet* design also gives you an added benefit: you can model your data in a one-to-one relation to the database—model it physically—or you can create different, logical relations that do not mirror the physical database—model it logically.

ADO.NET is made of more than merely two classes—actually the classes span several namespaces including:

- *System.Data*: Contains classes that are primarily used to contain and manipulate data, such as the *DataSet* and the *DataTable* classes.
- *System.Data.Common*: Contains set of classes that provide functionality common to the other ADO.NET namespaces.
- *System.Data.OleDb*: The OLEDB .NET data providers. These classes provide the means to connect to any OLEDB data source, issue SQL queries (database query commands), perform database transactions, etc.
- *System.Data.SqlClient*: Mirrors the *System.Data.OleDb* namespace and its classes but is optimized for working with Microsoft SQL Server.
- *System.Data.SqlTypes*: Provides data types that are native to Microsoft SQL Server, again this is an optimization.

Combined these classes provide a flexible, powerful way to work with data in .NET—whether from a database, data only created and kept during a program's lifespan, or from files.

Window Forms

Much of the press and marketing stress .NET as a development platform for Web solutions. The fact is that the .NET Framework is also the evolutionary next step to Windows and traditional application development. The `System.Windows.Forms` namespace provides the user interface elements specific to building dynamic, user-centric applications. It also unites the disparate Microsoft programming models, namely the Visual Basic Forms model, Microsoft Foundation Classes and the Windows application programming interfaces (Win32 APIs) to offer you a unified programming model that you can leverage from any of the .NET languages.

Windows Forms, as the name suggests, provides the means to do form based development. That is, you create each application interface—window or dialog—based on a `Form` control upon which you add other user interface elements, such as buttons, list boxes, edit boxes, etc. If you have experience with Visual Basic you will find yourself at home using Windows Forms. The `System.Windows.Forms` namespace contains an entire library of rich interface controls that you need and expect, including:

- `Button:` Represents a button control.
- `CheckBox:` Represents a check box control.
- `ComboBox:` Represents a combo box control; used to show multiple choices in a single column, drop down list-like format.
- `DataGrid:` Similar to a ListBox except it is a grid used to display data retrieved and contained by one of the many ADO.NET classes.
- `Form:` Represents a window or dialog upon which other controls are placed.
- `ImageList:` Used to contain and manage a group of images.
- `Label:` Displays a text or graphic label.
- `ListBox:` Represents a list box control. Displays data data in a single or multi-column format.
- and much, much more.

All the Windows Forms controls are derived from a common base class, `Control`, from which they inherit a general set of properties and methods. This makes using the controls more intuitive and creates consistency between the various controls. `Height`, `Width` and `BackColor` are examples of three of the seventy or so properties that all elements inherit from the `Control` class. As with most classes in .NET, you can inherit from the Windows Forms controls to create your own custom elements.

The striking similarity to Visual Basic 6 development model will make getting up to speed with Windows Forms fairly easy for many.

Note

Forms are just user interface elements—windows—upon which you drag and drop or programmatically create user controls, such as buttons and list boxes. It is quite similar to user interface design in Visual Basic 6.

ASP.NET

.NET actually provides an evolutionary step toward building Web-based applications with the introduction of ASP.NET. This is an enhancement of Microsoft Active Server Page (ASP) technology and among other things it introduces a new way to create Web solutions using Web Forms.

Note

Web forms and ASP.NET are *not* exactly synonymous. Each Web form is composed of an HTML page—an .aspx (ASP.NET) file—and an associated C# file that contains non-HTML server-side code to execute on behalf of the page. The visual Web form is actually a only a rendering of the final HTML page by Visual Studio .NET, making it possible to design your Web page visually.

Web Forms borrow the same idea of form-based programming found in Visual Basic as do Windows Forms, but it applies to Web development. The combination of Windows Forms and Web Forms offer you the same unifying development concepts and techniques for building interactive applications within .NET—the Form. This makes it easier for .NET developers to become proficient at building both Windows applications and Web solutions. Although these two types of solutions require different classes (the Web Forms namespace is System.Web.UI), the classes themselves have a great deal of similarity in concept, naming, features and how you use them.

Note

When you program Web solutions you must consider many issues that are different than when you develop desktop applications. The biggest difference is that the Web is a disconnected request and response model.

Note

Use ASP.NET and Web Forms to drag-and-drop your Web application interface using the same concepts as with Windows Forms.

ASP.NET, however, does not advance ASP or Web programming only by introducing the Web Forms. The most significant change from ASP is a technique called Codebehind, which makes it possible for you to separate your user interface and from your business logic. Unlike ASP, in which the page contains both the presentation code (HTML/ASP controls) and the logic (which uses scripting code), ASP.NET lets you separate the two. The interface code to display is contained in an .aspx file (the "x" tells the ASP server that it is a ASP.NET page) that can include a Codebehind reference to the code that executes the business rules.

The following code excerpt is the first line of an aspx file and shows you how the Codebehind declaration associates the the presentation layer with a business logic laye—contained in the C# file "WebForm1.aspx.cs":

```
<%@ Page language="c#" Codebehind="WebForm1.aspx.cs" AutoEventWireup="false"
➥Inherits="QueWeb.WebForm1" %>
```

There are several advantages to this separation of presentation and business logic. Generally, if you handle designing the Web interface you are most likely not the same person that creates the business logic. Because the interface and logic are separate files, they can be updated simultaneously by different users. Also, there is little risk in the graphic designer accidentally breaking the application logic code by inadvertently deleting something, and vice versa.

Another benefit of ASP.NET is that you do not have to write the code associated with the Web page in JScript or VBScript; you can use your choice of language— C#, Visual Basic .NET or any other .NET language. A secondary bonus to choosing your language of choice is that because the Codebehind is compiled processing is significantly increased.

Note

The Codebehind file is compiled when the .aspx page is served to the client browser. The code may be compiled just-in-time or precompiled and stored on the server.

ASP.NET also brings many other advantages compared to ASP—or any alternative—such as improved security, session state management, the ability to perform live updates on pages that are in use and the ability to deliver Web services (more on ASP.NET and Web services in Chapter 7, "Web Services").

Summary

This chapter introduced some basic concepts required for understanding the .NET Framework class library, as well as covered the vast amounts of functionality the library has, albeit one of more breadth than depth. You learned that the .NET Framework library is fully object oriented with its entire object rooted in the aptly named Object. You gained some understanding of the benefits of an object-based library and learned some of its features. To gain a true understanding of the class library warrants a book unto itself and is left to you to discover from the framework reference if you are inclined.

Common
Language
Runtime

Having learned some basics about the .NET framework classes, you can now look at the common language runtime. In this chapter, you'll learn how .NET executes its coded orders in order to make the .NET world possible.

What's a Runtime?

At the most basic level, a *runtime* is the execution environment upon which your software runs. It generally makes operating system services available to your programs, such as starting up and stopping threads and processes and satisfying any dependencies that one component has on any other component. Depending on the runtime, it might also manage memory, enforce security policies, manage file access, and determine how programs behave and interact with one another and the system upon which they are run.

Examples of Other Runtime Environments

Runtime engines exist for every programming language, but they vary in availability and features depending on the operating system. Some runtimes are available only on Microsoft Windows such as the VBRUN runtime of the Microsoft Visual Basic environment and the MSVCRT runtime that executes Microsoft Visual C++ programs. Other runtimes, such as the Java virtual machine (commonly known as the JVM) exist on multiple operating systems.

To get a better idea of how these runtimes differ, consider that the JVM and VBRUN both have automatic memory management, whereas the MSVCRT leaves the developer to handle this. What most every runtime has in common is that it executes programs written only in one specific language; you cannot run Visual Basic programs on the MSVCRT or the JVM.

How Is the Common Language Runtime Different?

What really sets the .NET platform apart from most every other platform is that it provides a unified runtime environment across a multitude of programming languages. Unlike Java, for instance, the .NET runtime can execute programs written in *any* language that meets its common language specification. Hence, the name *common language* runtime. As you will learn, this also means that programs written in one language can call programs or components written in other languages, thus extending both the life of existing solutions and the productivity of developers whose repertoire of languages is limited.

Overview of the Components Runtime

From a distance, the common language runtime looks like one entity that simply manages program execution. Figure 6.1 looks at the big picture; it lists the components of the common language runtime.

Common Language Runtime

Base Class Library Support		
Security Engine	...	
MSIL to Native Compilers (JIT)	Code Manager	Garbage Collector (GC)
Common Type System	Class Loader	Common Language Specification

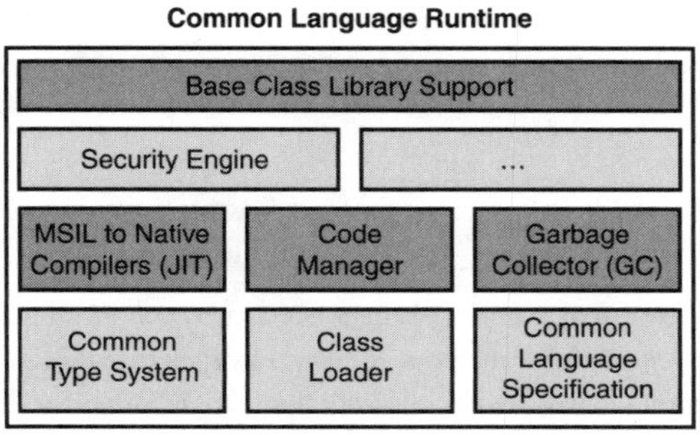

Figure 6.1

Components of the common language runtime.

As you can see from Figure 6.1, the common language runtime is composed of various components and services with different functional responsibilities, including:

- The common type system
- The common language specification
- The class loader
- The just in time (JIT) compiler(s)
- The garbage collector

The runtime also provides security services, manages threading, and provides the profiling and debugging services useful to programming.

The Common Type System

One of the goals of .NET, as you already know, is to offer developers the ability to choose the language that best meets their needs and knowledge base.

The common type system, which is arguably the centerpiece of the runtime, is one part of a two-pronged attack for making .NET cross-language compatible (see Figure 6.2)—the other is the common language specification. As the name, common type system, implies, it defines a set of rules and "qualities" that are common to most languages and make it possible for different languages to map into the .NET Platform (think: type framework). Some of the important aspects that the common type system are as follows:

- Includes rules for declaring, using, and managing types.
- Includes rules for implementing an object-oriented model within which most languages can be implemented.
- Includes rules for handling exceptions.
- Declares support for two categories of types (value and reference types).
- Establishes additional rules and regulations that make it possible to have cross-language integration.

Note

The common type system is not a running system but a collection of rules that the runtime execution engine applies as code runs. The execution engine creates a virtual execution system (VES) that implements the common type system, as well as garbage collection, instantiating the JIT, and managing all other aspects of code execution under the runtime.

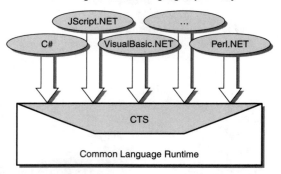

CTS Brings Us Cross-Language Operability!

Figure 6.2

The common type system makes cross-language compatibility possible.

As you might know, most languages have a great degree of overlap in the types of data they support (such as floating point numbers, integers, strings, and the like). The differences are mainly in how these types are physically represented and the restrictions on the values they can represent. For instance, although most languages have integers some only represent them using 16 bits and declare that they are unsigned in value. Other languages can have 16-bit integers but of signed value, and other languages can even have types to represent integers of 16-bit, 32-bit, and 64-bit lengths. Taking a concrete example, a C/C++ integer (`int`) on the Intel platform is 32-bits in size and is signed. Visual Basic, in contrast, has an integer type (`Integer`) that is 16 bits long.

Note

The number of bits determines the range of values that the type can represent. A 32-bit unsigned integer, for example, can represent 4,294,967,296 values whereas a 16-bit unsigned integer can only represent 65,536.

Resolving the differences in types and providing a mapping between various types is the first step towards supporting different languages. The type system strictly defines the permissible types and gives language creators the means to map their language types to the specifications (that is, the framework).

The type system also sets the rules for how value types and reference types are represented, created, and managed. Suffice it to say that value types and reference types are handled by the runtime differently and exhibit different characteristics.

Note

Incompatibility of types is one reason that most development environments and runtimes support only one or two programming languages. Microsoft Visual C/C++, for example, supports programming in C and C++, which are sibling languages. The Visual Basic development environment and runtime, on the other hand, only support Microsoft Visual Basic.

The common type system is one specification that makes a language-neutral system possible. The second is the common language specification, discussed next.

Defining the Common Language Specification

The common language specification complements the common type system by agreeing on a common set of language specifications that languages and tools must follow in order to be compliant. Compliance assures that a program written in a language will behave in a well-defined and understood manner. For example, instantiation of objects and method invocation adhere to a common set of rules; and value and reference types behave in a standard way. It is only through compliance to the specification that cross-language method invocations (having a program or component written in one language call an operation in a program written in another language) are guaranteed. For a less abstract example, consider the fact that the .NET Framework library is written in C#. How can a developer then use JScript or Eiffel to build a .NET solution without such rules? The answer, of course, is it would not be possible.

Note

Making a language compliant with the common language specification may require modifications to the language. The changes made to Visual Basic to make it a first-class citizen of .NET is a good example because it required numerous alterations. Even so, it is still "VB." JScript .NET, in contrast, required much fewer modifications.

Although the language specification is not part of the type system, strictly speaking, it is a subset of the type system and sets forth usage conventions. The specification is designed to be broad enough to ensure that as many languages as possible *can* be compliant in that they can be modified to adhere to the specification. Languages that meet this set of requirements are considered compliant. The same compliance comparison holds true for tool vendors; in order for code generated by a tool to be executable as managed code in .NET, it needs to meet the specification.

Note

Code that complies with the common language specification and executes within the .NET common language runtime is said to be *managed* code. Because it adheres to the specification, the runtime can fully manage its execution.

Creating a common type system and common language specification enables tool vendors and language designers to easily examine their language and do whatever is necessary to make the language tool comply.

Note

There is also what is known as *unmanaged* code, which takes into account that you as a developer might want to use features of a language that are not or cannot be managed by the common language runtime. For instance, because the garbage collector cannot manage memory that it does not allocate or deallocate, C/C++ pointers are not permissible under normal (managed) execution. This does not, however, mean that you cannot write or run C/C++ code that uses pointers. There is a way to declare and run code as unmanaged, which means that it is run outside of the runtime—you take responsibility for your code not leaking memory and not performing access violations.

A language or tool that meets the requirements of these common specifications makes it possible for developers to leverage their knowledge. It empowers them with the freedom and flexibility to use the tools and languages they feel best address the problems they need to solve.

Note

It is worth noting that the code emitted by common language specification-compliant tools must provide *metadata* that describes information about the types. This information includes which classes exist in the code, methods, what inheritance exists, code access security settings, and other information that the runtime needs in order to manage code execution.

It is precisely because of the common type system and common language specification that, at the time of this writing, there are well over two dozen languages either available on .NET or in the pipeline. Some of the languages already available include: C# (C-sharp); Visual Basic .NET; Microsoft Visual C++ with managed extensions; JScript .NET; Eiffel# (Eiffel-sharp); Smalltalk; Perl; COBOL; and Scheme.

Understanding the Garbage Collector

The common language runtime contains a great deal of functionality, employing numerous components to make .NET solutions run efficiently, stably, and secure. One of the most important aspects to that end is the garbage collector.

In order to address some of the development issues that plague stability and security of some languages and systems today, the .NET framework employs sophisticated memory-management techniques for both allocating and releasing memory when an application is running (the application's lifetime). Although the programmer still makes memory allocation requests, the runtime system employs a garbage collector to handle memory deallocation. Having the system take over responsibility for reclaiming unused memory increases stability and security. Recall that improper, untracked, or absence of deallocation can introduce access violations and memory leaks. In .NET, the garbage collector takes over the role of deallocation in several ways, all of which rely on it keeping track of references to objects.

Conceptually, when no references to an object exist, the garbage collector reclaims the memory. In practice, the only guarantee you have is that if there are no additional references to an object, it will collect the memory at some point in time. In other words, memory is not necessarily reclaimed at the first possible moment. Because the garbage collector does not guarantee when it will reclaim unused memory, programmers cannot and should not make any assumptions about the state of memory, which is generally good programming practice.

The reason that a delay in collecting the *garbage* (unused memory) can occur is because memory reclamation is an expensive system operation. By queuing the collection operations degradation in system performance is limited. This contrasts greatly with other runtime environments that recycle memory as soon as possible.

Note

C/C++ developers might not be pleased with the inability to control when and how memory is freed. However, all but a few programmers mishandle memory, especially when it comes to writing and calling memory destructors.

.NET aims to become the enterprise-level development and runtime platform of the future and stability is tantamount to this goal. Enterprise applications need to run for months, if not years, without hiccups or restarts. One way to ensure this result is to take the black art of memory management out of developers' hands; the system is certainly more capable than any developer of managing memory!

Increased Development Productivity

Stability is an obvious benefit of including a garbage collector in the runtime, but the increased programmer productivity is also a key advantage. By taking memory management out of human hands, there are simply fewer things for you to worry about when coding and less time is spent fixing code bugs. To that end, the garbage collector increases developer productivity.

Note

Some software projects designate a programmer/quality assurance specialist whose sole job is to track down and fix memory problems. Consider how much more productive your team would be if that person could be used elsewhere.

Using Just In Time Compiling

Now that you have learned a few of the feature components under the common language runtime's hood, you can learn about the one with the most inappropriate name: the just-in-time (JIT) compiler. .NET programs are not compiled directly into executable code but are compiled into an intermediary language known as Microsoft Intermediary Language (MSIL or IL). This language is compiled and executed later (see Figure 6.3). You may have heard of JIT compiling or "the JITer" from Java, but the similarity between .NET and Java stops abruptly at the term.

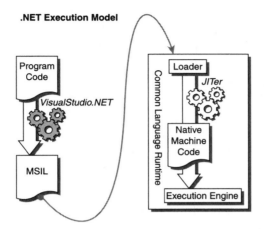

Figure 6.3

The .NET execution model—JIT compiling.

To better understand what JITing in .NET is all about, first consider a solution that does not use .NET. If you develop a solution using Visual C++ the output of the compilation process is machine code that is native to the targeted processor/ system and is directly executable. A traditional Windows program, for example, would have an .EXE file that you can double-click to make it run.

In .NET, things are a little different. Because .NET aims for optimization and the ability to run on any device, the compiler emits the program in an intermediary language known as Microsoft intermediate language (MSIL or IL). Essentially this is a processor-agnostic program that cannot run as is. When you run the program, the common language runtime loads the code into the runtime environment and a just-in-time compiler (JITer) compiles the IL into *native* executable code. This native code is then executed by the runtime's execution engine.

Benefits of JIT Compiling

The most obvious benefit of the common language runtime's JIT scheme is that it takes system-agnostic IL code and compiles it into native code for the system upon which it is running. This means that if you take a .NET program and run it on a four-way symmetric Itanium system, the runtime will optimize the code for that 64-bit processor. On the other hand, if you run that same code on an older Pentium II 300 MHz-based system, .NET will tailor that same IL code to the Pentium II's instruction set!

Like the garbage collector, the just-in-time process is optimized to make code run as efficiently as possible. It compiles code only when it needs to execute the code. The just-in-time compiler also caches compiled code to reduce the need to continuously recompile the same code every time it is called.

Note

It is possible for you to pre-just-in-time compile your entire .NET application. The advantage, however, is arguable because, although your program will initially execute faster, this speed advantage wanes over time. Rcall that normally the just-in-time compiler caches code it compiles. Once the compiler has "touched" the more frequently executed pieces of the solution no additional compilation is necessary and the advantage of pre-just-in-time compilation becomes negligible.

How Is It Different Than Java's JVM?

An important distinction between how .NET executes code and Java's use of a JITer is worth mentioning. On the Java platform, a just-in-time compiler is used to transform the Java program into platform-independent code known as *byte code*. In great contrast to .NET, byte code is not an intermediary language that is compiled to native, hardware optimized code, but is instead interpreted at execution time by the Java virtual machine. This process of interpreting code as it executes it is much slower than the compile-and-cache method used by the .NET JITer.

Considering Security

Although the framework provides security mechanisms, such as exists in the `System.Security` and related namespaces, it is the job of the runtime to ensure the set policies are adhered to. In .NET there are two types of security used by the runtime: *code access* and *role-based* security. In both cases, the runtime essentially counters security permission requests with responses. In understanding security, it is important to first understand the different types of permissions.

Permissions

Permissions-based security uses the notion of security permission requests and grants. The code requests the permissions it requires (or wants) and the runtime is responsible for validating that the code has the authority to receive such permissions. It does this by checking the security policy set by the administrator.

There are three types of *permissions*: code access, identity, and role-based permissions, as defined here:

- **Code access permissions:** Used to protect resources. Code can request permission to access a resource and it is the runtime's job to grant or deny the permission.

- **Identity permissions:** Granted when an assembly is loaded and the presented evidence validates against the required credentials. There are five identity permissions:

  `PublisherIdentityPermission`: The digital signature of software developer.

  `SiteIdentityPermission`: The Web site where the code originated.

  `StrongNameIdentityPermission`: Uniquely identifies an assembly using a strong name, which is composed of the assembly's text name, version number, culture information, a public key and a digital signature.

  `URLIdentityPermission`: The fully qualified originating URL.

  `ZoneIdentityPermission`: The originating zone (Microsoft Internet Explorer security zone).

- **Role-based security permissions:** Provide the means for determining whether a user or user agent belongs to a specific role or has a certain identity.

Note

Code and identity permissions have the same set of functionality and as such share a common base class: `CodeAccessPermission`.

Code Access Security

The runtime performs security checks before code is executed by analyzing the metadata and comparing the access requests to the system settings and during JIT compilation. For instance, one important component of code access security is verifying that code is type-safe. The JIT compiler examines the metadata and IL and if it determines that the program does not attempt to access memory locations outside its scope the code is type-safe. For example, object A does not access private (data) members of an object B. Because type-safe verification guarantees that the runtime can isolate an assembly, it makes it possible to load and execute multiple programs in the same process.

Note

Type-safe code accesses memory in well-defined and allowable ways. Code that accesses arbitrary computer memory location, for example, is not type-safe. Requiring code to be type-safe prevents accidental or malicious memory corruption.

Unlike application development today, .NET also enables programmers to declare the security access their programs require—either for the program itself or for programs calling upon it. These settings can be made globally (for the entire program) or in a local manner. The latter permits fine-tuned security. For instance, a class can have permissions set on itself or on its methods and members, thus declaring which security permissions are required by programs to manipulate or gain functionality of the code. The runtime ensures that the security settings are adhered to during execution (when the code is called before the JITer emits the code to execute) by "walking the call stack." The runtime not only checks the caller but the caller of the caller. The "walk" is performed all the way up the call chain to ensure that everyone involved, not just the immediate caller, has permission.

Role-Based Security

Role-based security is similar in idea to the security used in Windows today. You can create roles and assign permissions to them. Roles in turn can have one or more principles assigned to them and one or more roles can be assigned to a given principle. A principle simply represents an identity and acts on behalf of a user (a principle can also be a user in the Windows NT or 2000 security concept). The system administrator creates the security policies that determine which permissions a role is granted.

Security Policy

Security policy is the set of rules that the common language runtime follows when determining if it should grant permission(s) to code. Similar to security groups in Windows NT or Windows 2000, the security code groups have default permissions which administrators can tailor.

The runtime features has a security policies model that encompasses different elements:

- **Security levels:** The policy levels are enterprise, machine, user and application domain.

- **Code group hierarchies:** A subset of security policy levels, code groups are a logical grouping of code that defines permissions and the requirements for membership in the group.

- **Permission sets:** Several sets of permissions exist that you or an administrator can associate with code groups. The permission sets include `Nothing`, `Execution`, `Internet`, `LocalIntranet`, `Everything`, and `FullTrust`.

- **Evidence:** Information the runtime uses to make security policy decisions. You can custom design evidence or use one of the default types: Application directory (the solution's installation directory); digital signature of the publisher; cryptographic hash; zone of origin, such as IntranetZone; or originating Uniform Resource Locator (URL).

The common language runtime helps enforce the extensive security features that enable developers and administrators to manage security. The ability for developers to specify the code-access security they need to execute part or all of their code makes securing systems easier for administrators and makes it easier for developers to ensure that their code will function in the way they intend. For example, if your solution absolutely requires access to the computer's hard drive you may specify the appropriate security level. If the end user or administrator does not grant such permission, then it is clear that the access denial is the "failure," not the code per-se.

Having the ability to set within code the security required of calling classes or programs is not present in Windows, the MacOS or any Unix flavors. These features, coupled with the ability to custom-tune security from the administrative level, give .NET solutions a leg up on the competition. Granted, the Java platform does offer byte-code verification by the JVM, which is the capability to digitally sign code- and policy-based security. It does not have evidence-based security, nor the ability to stipulate permissions at the code access level.

Additional Runtime Services

While the common language runtime is not, strictly speaking, an operating system, it is the execution environment for all .NET applications and therefore exposes the services of the underlying operating system. The list of services that the common language runtime makes available is extensive and is purposely omitted here; however, there are a few additional notable services of which you should be aware:

- **Threading**—The runtime also encapsulates, exposes, and manages the threading model of the underlying operating system to .NET applications in an object-oriented way. This makes it easy to write applications that take full advantage of the OS features.

- **Exception Model**—The runtime has its own exception-handling model that is integrated with the exception model of the underlying operating system and the exception features of the respective programming languages. This enables you to use a consistent exception model across the entire .NET Platform.

- **Debugging and Profiling**—To make developing optimized solutions easier, the framework ships with a code profiler that can be attached to the common language runtime. The profiler then logs performance events, such as the number of CPU cycles burned by a particular method, as well as detailed information useful for stabilizing an solution, such as which system exception occurred and its cause (that is, who threw the exception and when). In a similar manner of convenience, a debugger can be attached to a running application.

The AppDomain

If you are more technically inclined, understanding the runtime in action will make you better aware of some its additional benefits. What happens behind the scenes when running a .NET application is actually similar to what happens when running a Win32 application on Windows.

What is known as the runtime host actually has the responsible for loading the common language runtime. There are three hosts aimed at handling three usage scenarios. There is an ASP.NET host for running Web solutions, a Microsoft Internet Explorer host for running browser controls, and a shell executable host for running executables (such as Windows programs).

The order of events is that an operating system process is created that starts up the appropriate host. This host in turn loads the common language runtime, which in turn creates an application domain. Application domains (`System.AppDomain`) are the runtimes' version of an operating system process (just like the one hosting the runtime host) and provide an isolated space in which an application can run. The runtime creates one application domain per application and each domain can spawn additional domains (see Figure 6.4).

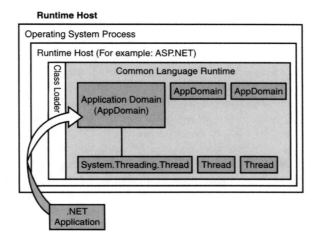

Figure 6.4

The runtime host and its relation to the common language runtime and AppDomains.

Additionally, similar to an operating system, an AppDomain is free to spawn threads as required. Interestingly, the common language runtime runs AppDomains on a single thread but there is no one-to-one association between threads and AppDomains. At any given time, any given thread can be running in any given AppDomain or be used to run any other AppDomain, as illustrated in Figure 6.5. At any given interval, the Thread-AppDomain association may change.

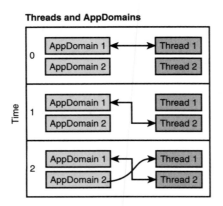

Figure 6.5

Relation between the AppDomain and threads.

Summary

The .NET common language runtime is responsible for managing code execution for the .NET Platform. Its combination of features provides a robust environment upon which solutions written in any language compliant with the common language specification can run. Because of this, your developers can leverage whichever of the many available .NET-compatible languages they know best to get up and running quickly. Such features as advanced garbage collection make development more efficient because they enable programmers to concentrate less on "the art" of memory management and more on getting features complete. The GC also helps you and your team produce stable software the first time around, thus saving time and costs on quality assurance testing. These features of the runtime, coupled with its particular flavor of JIT execution of code, make it a compelling runtime—and make .NET what it is.

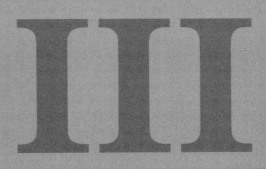

Web Services
Explored and
Explained

7

Web
Services

As you learned in Chapter 3, "Why .NET?," a Web service is similar to a service in the real, physical world. Software solutions are by definition services: they provide the answers to problems; they automate tasks; they facilitate daily work; they calculate the otherwise incalculable; and more. However, the notion of building deliverable software that is either pushed to or pulled from a desktop PC or handheld device has only become possible because of the advent of the Web. Its wide acceptance and availability makes it the ideal delivery infrastructure for software services.

The fact that the Web is built on solid, open technologies that are operating-system neutral only solidifies its position as the preferred platform. The primary technologies underlying the Internet are the HyperText Transfer Protocol (HTTP) and HyperText Markup Language (HTML). However, as Web services are less about interactive Web pages and more about transparent services, Microsoft and other companies have worked together under the auspices of the World Wide Web Consortium (also known as the W3C) to define the additional technologies necessary. These include:

- The eXtensible Markup Language (XML)
- Web Services Description Language (WSDL)
- Simple Object Access Protocol (SOAP)
- Universal Description, Discovery, and Integration (UDDI)

Note

To learn more about the World Wide Web Consortium, visit the W3C Web site at www.w3c.org.

You will learn more about each of these technologies and its role and/or influence in .NET in the sections ahead.

The Web Technologies Behind Web Services

Web services would obviously not be possible without the Web to make them accessible. However, the Web is not just conceptually important to Web services—a 100% available network that is publicly accessible—but practically important. That is because the Web defines a standard that is not controlled by any one company or interest and as such is open not just in terms of access but in terms of technology. The open standards that were defined for the Web and are used to make it a reality are what makes universal Web services possible.

This chapter will touch upon the various technologies that lie behind the scenes and are the plumbing of the Web and also highlight how those technologies apply to Web services. Feel free to skim through some of these sections as they may be "old hat" to you, such as HTML, while sections will certainly introduce you to new information.

HyperText Transfer Protocol (HTTP)

The globally accessible information-at-your-fingertips Web is made possible by two technologies: HyperText Transfer Protocol (HTTP) and HyperText Markup Language (HTML). HTML is known as an application layer transport protocol and, technically speaking, simply defines a message-based architecture for making resource requests and fulfilling them. The design goal of HTTP is to provide the means to build distributed information systems. The underling motivation was to make it possible to not only share information but to collaborate. As such, HTTP was designed as a generic, stateless, protocol so that it's use might be as wide and diverse as possible.

Although you do not need to know the details, it is helpful to understand that the request/response message format is simple and neatly contained in a small set of predefined messages: GET, PUT, POST, HEAD, DELETE, CONNECT, OPTIONS, and TRACE. Because it is designed to be a generic protocol it does not specify how to present data—it is like a ferry operator, able to carry a multitude of payloads from point to point. For these reasons, it was chosen as the protocol for the Web, which is undoubtedly the single largest deployment of HTTP.

Choosing to build Web services atop HTTP makes sense not only because it is an open standard but also because it is open in nature. To facilitate building distributed information systems, the .NET platform was built atop HTTP and is the default protocol underlying the system. Within the .NET Framework, you will find an entire namespace, System.Web, devoted to HTTP. Because the common language runtime uses the HTTP classes to implement its own HTTP server that is used by/for ASP.NET, it facilitates building and delivering Web applications and services.

HyperText Markup Language (HTML)

Whereas HTTP is a protocol for delivering information, the HyperText Markup Language (HTML) is designed for presenting it. Essentially, HTML is a presentation programming language whose instructions are comprised of a predefined set of "tags" that tell your Web browser how to display the information on your screen. For example, the <H> tag is used to mark text between the opening tag, <H>, and the closing tag, </H>, as a heading. Most browsers will render the text in a larger, bold font to make it stand out.

```
<H> Joe Black </H>
```

The HTML tags are also used to create links to and between documents or words. Additionally, there are tags that either wholly import information (such as images) or create selectable links (hyperlinks) to other sections in the document or another document entirely. There are tags for creating tables and lists and tags have attributes, such as `color` or `background` color. HTML gives authors the means to apply formatting and the "tools" to link information.

Note

The Web browser is a presentation engine that handles the rendering of the Web page on whatever device it is running, whereas HTML is the instruction set (program code) that instructs it.

The end goal of HTML and Web browsers is to make it possible to view information in the most device-independent manner as possible. The platform-neutral nature of HTML is a driving force behind the explosion of Web-based applications. For this obvious reason, .NET incorporates support for building HTML-based Internet and intranet applications.

.NET actually provides an evolutionary step toward building Web-based applications by introducing ASP.NET. This is an enhancement of Microsoft Active Server Pages (ASP) technology and among other things it introduces a new way to create HTML pages: using Web forms.

Web forms borrow the idea of form-based programming found in Visual Basic and apply it to Web development. By doing this, there is one unifying development concept for applications with a user interface in .NET—forms. This makes it easier for .NET developers to become proficient at building both Windows applications—using .NET's Windows Forms—and Web solutions—using .NET Web Forms. Although these two types of solutions require different classes and have slightly different programming considerations, the classes themselves have a great deal of similarity.

Note

Web forms and ASP.NET are *not* exactly synonymous. Each Web form is composed of an HTML page—an .aspx (ASP.NET) file—and an associated C# file that contains non-HTML server-side code to execute on behalf of the page. The visual Web form is actually a design-time rendering of the HTML page by Visual Studio .NET, making it possible to design your Web page visually.

eXtensible Markup Language (XML)

The eXtensible Markup Language (XML) is a sister language to HTML. Similar to HTML, XML uses tag notation; however, unlike HTML it is not restricted to a dictionary of terms. XML lets you define your own tags that have semantic meaning to you and your application. In this way, XML data is data about data—metadata.

Using the previous example in the HTML section, you can define a `<Name>` tag that is used to contain the customer's name. By doing this, when the data is passed to and from an application, the context of the data is preserved with the data itself. If, for example, you want to pass the customer's information to a Web browser, you can set up processing rules to take the XML `<Name>` data and format it using the HTML header tag.

Until XML came along, companies wanting to transfer data between their applications or between firms used proprietary data formats or the available standardized data interchange formats, such as X12 and UN/EDIFACT, which are complex and therefore costly to implement.

In contrast to other EDI formats, XML is not only a lingua franca but is easy to understand and work with. Because it is a text-based hierarchical structure, you can use it to communicate with *everything*.

Note

You can find the XML specification at `http://www.w3.org/TR/REC-xml`. The current version is 1.0 but don't expect it to change much if at all. Because XML is by definition extensible, it has and will continue to evolve through additional specifications that build on the framework XML 1.0 defines (XPath, XMLSchema, XLink, XForms, XSL/T, and so on).

Although XML enables you to define your own tags, the specification also gives a means of declaring which tags are permissible and which document structure is legal. This is done through the creation and use of document type definitions (DTDs) and/or XML schema (a separate XML-based specification). Both DTDs and XML schema are documents that define what elements can exist in an XML document and how they are related to one another. XML schema is a way to enforce the semantics that you define for your data. Your browser or application simply utilizes what is known as a *validating XML parser*, such as Microsoft's MSXML parser, to validate your XML document against one or more XML schema documents. If the rules set forth in the schema are adhered to, the XML document is considered valid.

Together, XML and XML schema are a foundation upon which additional XML-based specifications are built, such as SOAP and UDDI and are vital to making Web services possible. The .NET platform uses XML extensively and natively. Components of .NET such as ADO.NET use XML internally to represent all data and provide native input/output operations on data as XML documents. In this way, .NET uses XML to facilitate building Web services that access stored data. There is little need to "massage" or format data that your service needs to return to a customer—it's already in XML, which is what .NET Web services use to communicate information.

Simple Object Access Protocol (SOAP)

With XML and XML schema, you can define document structure and specify semantics in a way that lets you communicate data usefully. XML is text only; therefore, it is application- and firewall-friendly. HTTP certainly can be used as a protocol for sending and receiving XML documents, but when it comes to application integration across the wire—any network including your corporate local area network (LAN) or the Internet—where not only simple data but "object data" must be communicated, another XML technology enters the arena: the simple object access protocol (SOAP). SOAP is another open standard that Microsoft helped define (in conjunction with UserLand Software, International Business Machines Corporation, Lotus Development Corporation, DevelopMentor and other contributing companies and individuals).

As it is built atop XML and XML schema, SOAP is not only homogenously XML but extensible. The power of SOAP is that it is not only platform-agnostic but also transport-neutral. Currently SOAP is used in conjunction with Web servers and piggybacks on HTTP but its neutrality makes it useable on other protocols too (SMTP, for example). The goal of the protocol is to provide a method to make remote procedure calls (RPCs) and cross-application messaging.

The advantage of using SOAP is that unlike HTTP, which is limited in the types of data that it can describe, SOAP is designed for describing any and every data type. In distributed computing, one of the major challenges is calling methods/services remotely—on another computer over the wire. The technicality is not important to explain here, only that it is a challenge. There are solutions, such as DCOM (Distributed COM), but they are proprietary and require extensive network bandwidth. SOAP, on the other hand, solves the issues in an open, easily implementable manner, which is why it is a logical choice for use with Web services.

From the messaging side of things, SOAP is a self-describing XML data exchange container that you might find easiest to think of in postal terms: The XML instance document is the package contents and SOAP is the one size-fits-all envelope.

Note

If you are interested in learning more about the SOAP specification, the best place to look is *the* official SOAP 1.1 standards specification, which you can find at the W3C specification at http://www.w3.org/TR/SOAP/. For additional insight, you might find Microsoft's SOAP Web section of great use, especially from the standpoint of using Microsoft technologies. Point your browser to http://msdn.microsoft.com/library/default.asp and search for SOAP.

You might also find newtelligence AG's SOAP-related resources and "in-house" articles insightful. Point your browser to www.newtelligence.com and select the "news" menu; there you will find links to the following articles:

- "Catch Some SOAP —Building the Business Logic Backbone of the Internet," by Clemens F. Vasters
- "Why SOAP Doesn't Lack Security While It Does," by Clemens F. Vasters
- "Soap Chained Transactions (SOAP-CTX) Discussion Paper," by Clemens F. Vasters and James Snell

SOAP is the Web service protocol of choice in .NET. Obviously, having a platform-neutral format for exchanging data and coupling it with a way to exchange those documents is the foundation of Web services.

UDDI

.NET leverages a few additional XML-based technologies that are vital to delivering on the Web services promise. As you might imagine, creating a Web service that is callable remotely over a network is one part of the puzzle. The biggest task, though, comes when developers want to discover what Web services are out there. What they need, then, is a directory of Web services.

Microsoft, IBM, and other industry leaders came together to define such a directory of services. The fruit of that labor is the universal description, discovery, and integration (UDDI) specification, which defines "platform-independent, open framework for describing services, discovering businesses, and integrating business services using the Internet, as well as an operational registry that is available today." (See http://www.uddi.org/about.html for more information.) You can find an implementation of the UDDI framework at uddi.microsoft.com. Here you can enter your company name, contacts by department, contact information, a short overview of what your business does and, of course, information about and links to Web services you offer. It's an active Web services yellow pages (see Figure 7.1).

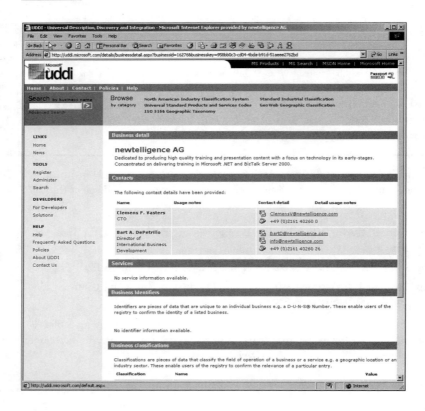

Figure 7.1

Corporate entry at the Microsoft UDDI Web services registry.

Because UDDI makes it possible for businesses to describe themselves and their services in a universally accessible and standardized way, businesses can then dynamically find each other and perform electronic transactions between their systems. Microsoft has a good FAQ on UDDI, which you can find at `http://uddi.microsoft.com/about/FAQbasics.aspx`. You can also learn more about UDDI by visiting either `http://www.uddi.org` or `http://uddi.microsoft.com`.

Note

The entire Microsoft UDDI Web site is running on ASP.NET, which is an active demonstration of Microsoft's faith as to the maturity and power of .NET.

WSDL and DISCO

Although UDDI provides a Registry mechanism for companies and their services, the Web Service Description Language (WSDL) is a technical interface description that UDDI can use. This markup language provides a means of describing your service, its semantics, and its call syntax and serves as the contract of the service. It uses a specific XML grammar to describe the structure of your Web service and specify the Web service "entry point"—which is the URL where others can find your service. You can discover a Web service description in .NET by calling upon a DISCOvery file (.disco). This is an XML-based document that makes it possible to discover Web services programmatically. Additionally, it describes the capabilities of the Web service and can provide resource links that further describe the service.

Note

For a detailed description of WSDL, check out the description on Microsoft's MSDN site (msdn.microsoft.com/net) or the W3C specification at http://www.w3.org/TR/wsdl.html.

Changing the Production/Consumption Paradigm

Web services have a big impact on consumers and producers of both software and traditional services. You learned in Chapter 3 about Web services in general and Microsoft .NET My Services in particular. Certainly, you might be wondering how you can use Web services and how producing or consuming them might prove different than traditional solutions development. This section addresses those issues.

Web Services: Tomorrow's Components

Part of that exploration might be in thinking about your existing software solutions and considering whether they might lend themselves to becoming Web services as a whole or a part of a solution. On the more traditional and innovative side, the notion of taking your business processes and digitizing them into universally accessible software services is enticing.

There is certainly a parallel between using Web services in this manner and in buying reusable COM/COM+ or JavaBean components. There are also distinct differences between developing and using traditional components and consuming and producing Web services.

Conceptually, you can think of Web Services as remotely residing software components that you call upon. Like COM or Java components, they have a defined "purpose" (the functionality they implement) and expose one or more interfaces that define the means of interacting with them. Interfaces are nothing more than the published methods upon which you call to deliver a service. The real difference is that, although components can conceptually be isolated, specialized pieces of code, they are seldom actually designed or implemented as stateless objects with atomic operations.

Note

Web services do not maintain any application state on behalf of the consumer. Each service is called to deliver a very specifically defined service and the service (or result) must be deliverable "as is." In other words, unlike traditional development you can't expect to call some methods that "set things" up and then call a "now give me the result" method. Everything must happen in one service call, so all information required by the service must be passed within the one (atomic) call.

For example, you can create a component that calculates interest on a loan and provides separate methods to set each value required by the calculation engine. There might exist the following:

- `SetInterestRate`, which sets the interest rate used in the calculation.
- `SetOutstandingLoanAmount`, which sets the amount of the loan.
- `SetPeriodOfTime`, which sets the period of time over which the calculation runs.
- `ReCalculateBalance`, which requests the outstanding balance be recalculated.

As you can see, each method has a distinct purpose but at least one method requires that a certain state of the component exist—you can't calculate it unless you have set the numbers beforehand. This fictitious component assumes certain things about how it will be used, which means that maintaining the object's or objects' state is not an issue. Although it is technically possible to create a Web service that behaves like this, you would not want to. Unlike a component that is most likely installed on each client computer, a Web service can have thousands of users consuming its service at any given time. Therefore, maintaining state is not advisable—do not think of Web services as simply components that are universally accessible via the Web.

You should also assume *nothing* about how your customers might consume your Web services, or that they will consume them in exactly the way you intended. Consumers often have different ideas about how to use a product than a manufacturer dreams up. And unlike components that often come with source code, consumers of your Web services will only have the description and callable methods you provide to work with, so the details must be clear. Behavior should be more predictable than your existing solutions based on your documentation.

Web services are promising and will come to have as prominent a place for developers and users as COM and Java components do today. However, issues related to security and authentication must be resolved. You must keep in mind that Web services are an evolving paradigm and best-cases models and patterns have yet to be invented. Sun, IBM, Microsoft and others might disagree on some of the backend infrastructure for realizing these services, but this is mostly from a development tool or runtime environment standpoint. All agree on and are involved in developing and promoting the underlying standards that are so important to making Web services universal and, from that standpoint, Web services are something to consider today.

Summary

Although *Think.NET* is about the Microsoft .NET platform, it is fair to point out that .NET is not the only Web services contender out there.

However, Because .NET was built from the ground up with Web services as an "application" target, the .NET framework comes with numerous classes aimed toward that end. The.NET framework library includes an extensive set of HTTP, HTML, XML, SOAP and other facilitators that makes it a premiere platform for building robust Web services, as well as other software solutions. It is a bag of goodies that makes development easier (if not better!) and enables you to produce software services more efficiently. Microsoft's decision to introduce .NET with a "from-the-ground-up" new version of Visual Studio that hooks into this infrastructure is the real threat to competing technologies from IBM, Sun, or others. Once you have taken Visual Studio .NET for the proverbial "test drive," you will not want to return it.

The development folks in Redmond have produced a cool tool with Visual Studio .NET, especially with the Enterprise Application Edition. You'll learn more about Visual Studio .NET in "The .NET Secret Weapon."

Suffice to say that it is an engineering wonder—development has never been so streamlined.

The only drawback might be that the tried-and-true, hard-core developers might feel too coddled by it. Even a beginner can get up and developing in little time. Both managers and practical developers will realize this is an advantage when it comes to delivering solutions on time.

ORCHESTRATION • SECURITY • NAM
VISUAL STUDIO .NET • JUST-IN-TIME
GARBAGE COLLECTOR • LANGUAGE
DENCE • COMMON LANGUAGE RUN
SERVICES • CLASS LIBRARY • .NET FI
ENTERPRISE SERVERS • MIGRATION •
ORCHESTRATION • SECURITY • NAM
VISUAL STUDIO .NET • JUST-IN-TIME
GARBAGE COLLECTOR • LANGUAGE
DENCE • COMMON LANGUAGE RUN
SERVICES • CLASS LIBRARY • .NET FI
ENTERPRISE SERVERS • MIGRATION •
ORCHESTRATION • SECURITY • NAM
VISUAL STUDIO .NET • JUST-IN-TIME
GARBAGE COLLECTOR • LANGUAGE
DENCE • COMMON LANGUAGE RUN

The Visual Studio .NET

Coinciding with the release of the .NET Platform is Microsoft Visual Studio .NET, the successor to the popular Visual Studio development tools suite. While Microsoft offers two versions of the tool, Visual Studio Enterprise Developer (VSED) and Visual Studio .NET Enterprise Architect (VSEA), this chapter focuses on the more comprehensive enterprise version.

Visual Studio .NET is the first compiler for Microsoft's new language, C# (pronounced "C-sharp"). More than just a compiler, the overhauled integrated development environment (IDE) is choc-full of features and tools to make developing any kind of solution imaginable easier—from console applications to Windows applications, from Web sites to Web services—Visual Studio .NET has it all. Version 7 of the ever-popular Windows development tool is a member of the .NET family; it includes wizards for ADO.NET (the successor to the ADO) and Windows Forms (the successor to MFC/traditional user interface-based Windows development).

This chapter includes an introduction to many of the features of the tool, where you'll gain a better understanding of how it can ease development for both experienced programmers and novices alike. This is not a "how to use Visual Studio .NET" lesson, which is outside the scope of this book. Instead, this chapter just "gets your feet wet" with the tool by outlining some of the major features that make the tool a development productivity center, especially .NET development.

Easing Developers into .NET

One of the most significant short-term productivity drains that a production team can encounter is when a new development tool is introduced. Certainly, coupling a new tool with one or more new languages, a new framework library, and a new philosophy is a significant combination to assault developers' with. Visual Studio .NET, like .NET itself, is all-new and Microsoft has taken apparent pains to make the transition as easy and productive as possible.

When using Visual Studio .NET, the first thing you might notice is that user orientation begins from the opening screen. When starting the tool you are greeted with a start page that contains tabs covering different topics such as "Get Started," "What's New," "Online Community," "Headlines," "Search Online," "Downloads," "Web Hosting," and "My Profile." The first time you run Visual Studio .NET the "My Profile" page is selected, which permits you to choose various environment settings, including several keyboard schemes and the layout of the application windows (see Figure 8.1) aimed at making the environment easier.

Note

The start page is actually an HTML page and as such you can customize it to better serve your development needs. For instance, you could have it display the most pressing bugs that developers need to address.

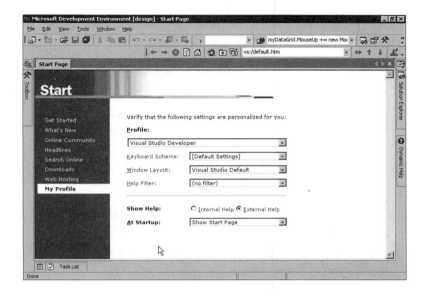

Figure 8.1

Users of previous Visual Studio versions might especially appreciate the availability of the various profiles—seven in all. These profiles allow you to set the keyboard shortcuts and the windows layout, making the IDE mimic other Microsoft development tools such as Visual Basic 6, Visual Studio C++ 6, and Visual InterDev Developer to name a few. In addition to selecting or customizing the keyboard you can also set the window layout separately.

- **Keyboard choices**: Default Settings; Visual Basic 6; Visual C++ 2; Visual C++ 6; or Visual Studio 6.
- **Windows Layout**: Visual Studio Default; Visual Basic 6; Student Window Layout; No Tool Windows Layout.

It is in the "My Profile" tab that you can also set the default startup page. This can be one of the following: Start page, last loaded solution, the Open dialog box, the New Project dialog box, or an empty environment. You can also set a filter for the dynamic help system (which is *very* cool and a real help) and select whether using the familiar "F1" key will call up the help system as a page within the IDE or externally (see Figure 8.2).

These customizations obviously make it possible for you and your team to get up to speed quickly.

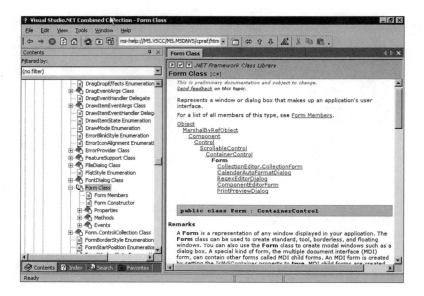

Figure 8.2

You can set help to come up within the Visual Studio .NET integrated development environment or externally using Microsoft Explorer.

Understanding Project Templates

Another way that Visual Studio facilitates your migration from previous platforms to .NET is through a comprehensive assortment of project templates. These are aimed at generating a basic project skeleton (or code template) that includes core functionality required by the type of project you are targeting. As you might know, project templates save you time developing solutions because the plumbing is done for you, freeing you to concentrate on developing your solution.

For instance, selecting to create a new project based on the C# console template generates a project that includes references to the .NET Framework namespaces you will need to use, a C# file that contains a code skeleton and a default assembly information file that you can customize. Although nothing special will happen, you can build and run the generated console "solution" without modification.

Because even the simplest of console applications uses system resources, the project contains a reference to the System namespace and the code must declare that it uses this namespace: using System.

Note

A *console application* is a solution that uses a text-based interface window, known as a console window, similar to old DOS or Unix applications. In other words, it has no graphics user interface or dialog boxes. These are mainly used to write backend code or small applications that test backend solution logic without the overhead of using a full graphics interface.

Although there is minimal front-end code generated when producing a console solution, the convenient inline comments that are inserted help orient you and hint at where to insert your custom code. The generator also provides directives that guide you as to where to modify the code in order to achieve certain behavior.

Selecting to create a new project from the Start page (or the File menu) presents you with the dialog box, shown in Figure 8.3. This dialog box gives you several template choices from which to base your application.

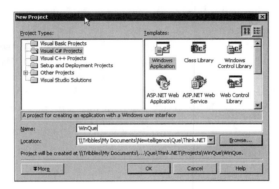

Figure 8.3

Easily create new projects using an available template.

As you can see, the available project templates are conveniently organized into six logical categories:

- Visual Basic projects
- Visual C# Projects
- Visual C++ Projects
- Setup and Deployment Projects
- Other Projects
- Visual Studio Solutions

The *Visual Basic Projects* (expect the name to change to Visual Basic.NET) and *Visual C# Projects* template groups consist of the following project types, specific of course to their respective languages:

- Windows Application
- Class Library
- Windows Control Library
- ASP.NET Web Application
- ASP.NET Web Service
- Web Control Library
- Console
- Windows Service
- Empty Project
- Empty Web Project
- New Project in Exiting Folder

Except perhaps for the *Empty Project* template, these are all .NET based. For example, the *Windows Application* template gives both C# and Visual Basic.NET solutions a forms-based application similar in "look and feel" to a Visual Basic 6 (forms) based solution but using the new *Windows Forms* namespace and its classes. This namespace essentially encompasses the Visual Basic 6 and Visual C++ Microsoft Foundation Classes (MFC)-based development into a unified forms-based solution.

On the other hand, if you have experience with the current Visual C++ 6, you will find most of the *Visual C++ Projects* familiar:

- ATL Project
- ATL Server Project
- ATL Server Web Project
- Custom Wizard
- Extended Stored Procedure DLL
- Makefile Project
- Managed C++ Application
- Managed C++ Class Library
- Managed C++ Empty Project
- Managed C++ Web Service
- MFC ActiveX Control
- MFC Application
- MFC DLL
- MFC ISAPI Extension DLL
- Win32 Project

Visual Studio .NET does not force you to migrate to .NET-based solutions immediately but empowers you to continue to create solutions based on the current C++-based Windows development technologies. You can still create ATL- or MFC-based projects because Visual Studio .NET also tucks under the rug the traditional Windows development power of Visual Studio 6. Selecting, for example, the *MFC Application* project template (see Figure 8.4) brings up a rather familiar looking MFC wizard.

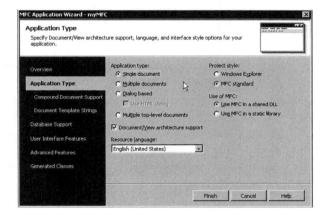

Figure 8.4

The newest version of the Microsoft Foundation Classes (MFC) is fully supported with wizards similar to the ones found in Visual Studio C++ version 6.

Note

Microsoft Foundation Classes (MFC) are a C++ based framework that facilitates building Windows solutions. Visual Studio complements the library with numerous wizards, making producing Windows applications easier and quicker.

You should note that the Visual Studio .NET team did not simply toss in Visual Studio's MFC framework library as an afterthought; this is a new version of MFC that supports the new controls and services that Windows XP introduces.

However, because Visual Studio .NET is *really* more about .NET than MFC or ATL, the Visual C++ project includes technology that will aid you in your transition to .NET and also aid you in migrating some of your existing solutions to .NET. Microsoft has added some extensions to the Visual C++ language, called *managed extensions*, which enable you to develop traditional Visual C++ solutions with some of the benefits that the managed world of .NET development offers.

The Visual Studio .NET team realizes that creating solutions is useless without getting them deployed! You will find several useful templates that aid you in getting your .NET solutions out into production by creating five templates toward this end. The *Setup and Deployment Projects* include the following:

- Cab Project
- Merge Module Project
- Setup Project
- Setup Wizard
- Web Setup Project

As you review the template names, you will see that you can install just about any sort of .NET or traditional Windows solution.

In what seems to be a placeholder for things to come, you will find the *Other Projects* group, which contains three sub-categories: *Database Projects, Enterprise Template Projects* and *Extensibility Projects*. You might expect this to also become the location of third-party templates. *Database Projects* contains one template, *Database Project*, and the *Extensibility Projects* contains a *Visual Studio .NET* add-in template and a *Shared* add-in template.

The *Enterprise Template* project group contains several templates for creating enterprise class solutions including:

- Visual Basic Simple Distributed Application
- Visual C# Simple Distributed Application
- Visual Basic Distributed Application
- Visual C# Distributed Application
- Distributed Application
- Enterprise Template Project

It also has two sub-groups: *Visual Basic Building Blocks* and *Visual C# Building Blocks*. These subgroups contain templates that differ only in the language they use; you can find the following templates:

- Business Façade
- Business Rules
- Data Access
- System
- ASP.NET Web Service
- WebUI

Lastly is the *Visual Studio Solutions* category, which contains a *Blank Solution* template for additional third-party templates.

Using the Integrated Development Environment (IDE)

After you choose the type of project you want to create and allow Visual Studio .NET to generate the appropriate files and dependencies, you will find yourself in an improved integrated development environment (IDE). Using the default environment as a reference, you will find several dockable windows that make project navigation and organization intuitive. There are numerous "views" that allow you to look at different aspects of your solution in various ways, organize available development features in a way that reduces clutter but makes the options readily available, open specialized information windows, and simply help make development easier, less confusing and more productive.

The *Solutions Explorer*, for example, lists all a project's files and file references in a logically structured tree view. You can show all the files or only view the essential code files. Another view that VisualStudio 6 developers will recognize is the *Class View*, which shows each class in the solutions and its methods and properties. This makes it possible not only to get an overview of classes but also to jump into a class at a specific place easier. For example, if you double-click a method name in the view you are transported to that method in the code window.

Note that all the available views in the new IDE can be docked to the edge of the Visual Studio workspace or undocked so that they can be freely positioned anywhere on your display. An additional welcomed feature is the ability to autohide individual tool windows and views. Enabling a window's autohide causes it to slide off-screen when not in use leaving only a small named tab along the border. Moving your mouse over the tab causes the view to reappear.

Because you can enable or disable each window's autohide behavior individually, you can set less frequently used windows to hide, while "pinning" often used windows in place to keep them in view. Autohide and dockable windows are just some of the ways that the new IDE gives you to personalize your development workspace and keep it organized.

In the toolbox, you'll find user interface elements for HTML or Windows based solutions that you can drag-and-drop right onto a HTML or Windows Form (the form development paradigm was extended to HTML development to provide a consistent development model). You can then easily lay out the element in a WYSIWYG designer that also lets you access and set the properties of any of the objects with ease. The toolbox also comes choc-full database-related components that make it possible to easily access any OLE DB data source or database using the .NET data providers and other classes composing the data-centric ADO.NET technologies.

Although these objects are drag-and-drop, they are not user interface components. The ADO.NET objects can be used client or server side and are designed to simplify the processes of connecting to a data source, retrieving data, and working with that data using a disconnected data model. ADO.NET is the evolutionary successor to ActiveX Data Objects (ADO) and, although the acronym is similar, there is no ActiveX whatsoever in ADO.NET.

The fact that Visual Studio .NET integrates traditional development and rapid application development (RAD) so well (even surpassing the ease of the Visual Basic 6 environment) is a real plus. The IDE and the underlying .NET infrastructure are as adept at developing server-side solutions as they are at enabling rapid development of user intensive client-side solutions.

Another convenient feature of Visual Studio .NET IDE is the built-in task list, which you might find familiar from some of Microsoft's other development and designer tools. Here you can enter open tasks to be completed by you or other developers. Unlike previous iterations of the tool, the Visual Studio .NET task list not only allows for general comments and tasks but also permits you to annotate code with comments using predefined keywords—TODO, HACK, and UNDONE—such as the following example.

```
private void button1_Click(object sender, System.EventArgs e)
{
    // TODO: Add the customer id verification code
    // ...
}
```

You can create new keywords with which to comment your program code (see Figure 8.5). The comment will then automatically appear in the task list pane of the IDE. This "autotask" feature is not only handy but also helps keep code comments consistent. You can create a standard set of production comments for your team to use, thus making it easy to find and open tasks.

The IDE also enables you to mark specific lines of text and add them to the task list. Performing this action is as simple as positioning the cursor and selecting to add a "task list shortcut." An easily distinguishable marker is inserted in the margin designating that a bookmark exists at the given line (see Figure 8.6). Just like bookmarks in HTML or Word files, if you click the bookmarked item in task list, it will automatically bring that file and line of code up in the code window.

Another useful task-list related feature is that all compile-time errors are automatically added to the task list. This makes it much easier to manage and tackle code errors.

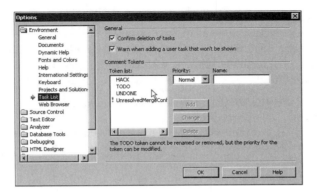

Figure 8.5

Create custom task list keywords that you can use to comment your program.

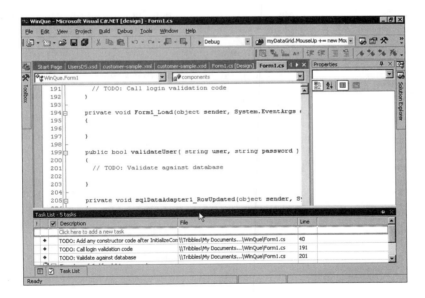

Figure 8.6

You can insert bookmarks into your code that appear in your task list. This gives you quick access to designated places in your program.

As if this were not enough for productivity and organization, Visual Studio .NET also includes a special comment syntax that enables the compiler to extract code comments to an XML file for later viewing, processing in Web reports, and for creating source code documentation. As with the comments, there is a set of predefined keywords (in this case XML-based) that you can use or extend (see Table 8.1).

Table 8.1   Specialized XML-Based Source Code Comment Keywords

XML Element	Description
c	Indicates code, but meant for single lines.
code	Counterpart to <c>; used to indicate multiple lines of code.
example	Inserts an example of how to properly use code.
exception	Documents a code exception.
include	References comments in another file.
list	Creates a formatted list.
para	Adds structure to a comment, not unlike the paragraph tag <P> in HTML notation. Used within another comment tag.
param	When commenting method calls, designates a parameter.
paramref	Gives you a way to indicate that a word is a parameter.
permission	Lets you document the permissions.
remarks	Meant to designate overview information.
returns	Indicates what is returned from a method.
see	Indicates a reference/link to other text.
seealso	Similar to the see element except that it references text to display in the See Also section.
summary	Describes a member of a type/class.
Value	Used to describe a property.

Understanding XML and the XML Designer

Like the rest of .NET, Visual Studio .NET is infused with XML technology. For one, you can use XML markup to facilitate the generation of code documentation. Visual Studio .NET also uses an XML parser—the Microsoft XML Parser (MSXML)—in its XML designer to enable you to edit XML with instant feedback. The designer allows you to create well-formed XML documents as well as validate documents against XML schemata.

There are several views for working with XML: one for working with XML documents in a structure source code fashion (the XML view); one for working with XML in a graphical hierarchy that is similar to many other XML editors (the Data view); and, lastly, an XML Schema view.

The XML editor will prove familiar to anyone who has done any XML-related development. Like many XML editors in circulation, there is dynamic *tag completion*, which automatically closes opening XML tags. This aids in making sure your documents are *well formed* (meaning that each XML beginning tag has an ending tag and that tags are properly nested according to the XML 1.0 specification).

The XML view facilitates quick and easy production of XML documents. However, Visual Studio .NET really steps into make development easier by allowing you to switch to a data view of your XML document. In this data view, you can review and work with XML data in a tabular manner similar to a database entry form. Each element that contains sub-elements appears as a table that you can enter data into directly. Now you can generate a general XML structure, such as the following:

```
<?xml version="1.0" encoding="utf-8" ?>
<NewDataSet xmlns="http://tempuri.org/XMLdoc.xsd">
<Customer>
  <FirstName></FirstName>
  <LastName></LastName>
  <Address>
    <Street></Street>
    <City></City>
    <State></State>
    <PostalCode></PostalCode>
  </Address>
</Customer>
```

Then, by switching to the data view (see Figure 8.7), anyone—even a non-technical person—can enter the data into the tables. The XML data document will be updated appropriately.

For example, if you enter two customers and then switch back to the XML view, Visual Studio .NET updates the file appropriately:

```
<?xml version="1.0" encoding="utf-8" ?>
<NewDataSet xmlns="http://tempuri.org/XMLdoc.xsd">
<Customer>
  <FirstName>Geoffrey</FirstName>
  <LastName>Bean</LastName>
  <Address>
    <Street>100 Devils Fiddle Road</Street>
    <City>Mordred</City>
    <State>NY</State>
    <PostalCode>01000</PostalCode>
```

```
    </Address>
  </Customer>
  <Customer>
  <FirstName>John</FirstName>
  <LastName>Doe</LastName>
  <Address>
    <Street>5 Grassling Lane</Street>
    <City>Middletown</City>
    <State>CT</State>
    <PostalCode>06710</PostalCode>
  </Address>
  </Customer>
</NewDataSet>
```

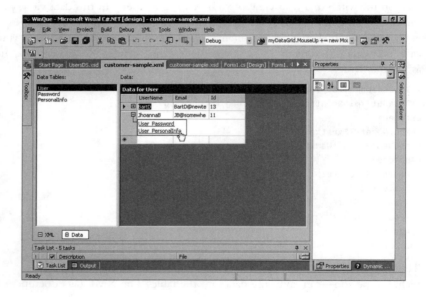

Figure 8.7

The data view allows you to enter XML-based data using a table view.

XML documents are most often generated by systems that transfer data from one module or application to another. Similarly, validation of XML documents, which is performed by comparing them to document type definitions (DTD) or XML Schemas (XSD), is also mostly done automatically and behind the scenes using a parser such as the MSXML parser. However, there are certainly times when you might need to hand-code an XML document and you will want to validate it against a schema. Visual Studio .NET includes the ability to validate dynamically what you code by hand in the XML view. By simply referencing your

XSD file or files from within your XML document (using the standard XML referencing mechanisms), the code editor will not only automatically and continuously validate the document against the schema but will also suggest valid elements using the improved Microsoft IntelliSense features.

In the previous example, if you were in the context of an `<Address>` tag and then typed a bracket (`<`), a context window would appear with the valid choices of `<Street>`, `<City>`, `<State>` and `<PostalCode>`. Should you ignore the choices and type some random tag, say `<dog>`, the system automatically would flag the error with a red squiggly underline similar to what Microsoft Word does when you make a spelling error. If you hover your mouse over the invalid tag, a context window pops up and tells you `"The active schema does not support the element..."` (see Figure 8.8). These are the types of features that make otherwise error-prone tasks straightforward and error-free.

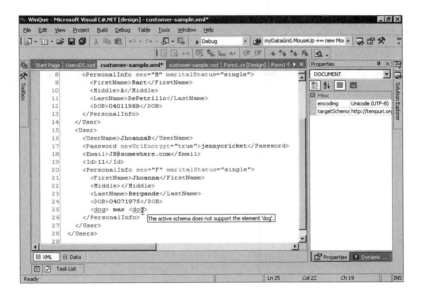

Figure 8.8

Microsoft IntelliSense gives you constant, helpful feedback when using Visual Studio .NET.

On the other side of the schema and validation equation is the case in which you create an XML document or are handed an existing one but have no corresponding schema (which often happens). You can automatically generate an XML schema using the `Create Schema` feature (see Figure 8.9). This feature not only generates the appropriate XSD file but also adds it to your project automatically and gives it the same name as your XML document.

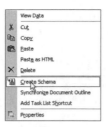

Figure 8.9

Use the Create Schema feature to create an XML schema (XSD) file from an XML document.

You can view the XML schema in two ways: Using the XML view or using the Schema view. The latter presents the schema in a graphical connected table view similar to an entity relation diagram common to most developers who have worked with databases. As you can see from Figure 8.10, you get a relational view of your XML schema—certainly a novel and useful option.

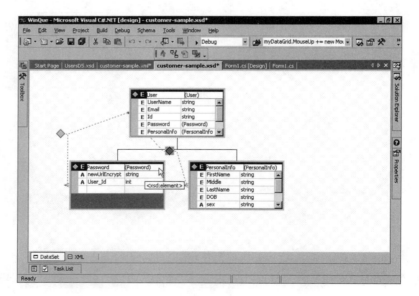

Figure 8.10

You can get a relational view of your XML schema similar to entity relation diagrams used for creating database schema.

Working with Databases

Another shining area for Visual Studio .NET and the underlying .NET Platform is when working with data, and especially databases. The .NET Framework provides a myriad data-related classes that facilitate working with information in a relational manner, whether your software uses a database, an XML file, or no data storage source or destination. Visual Studio .NET makes the entire data-centric processes easier by letting you access your data source from the IDE. You also can actually work directly with your database using the *Server Explorer* view. You simply need to navigate the tree to the *SQL Servers* node and then select an existing database to work with or create a new one (see Figure 8.11). For example, in Figure 8.11, you can see how easy it is to create a new database.

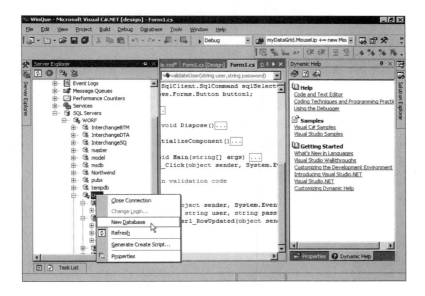

Figure 8.11

Creating a new database directly from the Visual Studio .NET Server Explorer window.

Creating a new database brings up a "Create Database" wizard, which lets you name the new database on the selected server and set the administrative name and password for the database server and database (see Figure 8.12).

Although the example connects to a Microsoft SQL Server 2000 database, you can as easily connect to an Oracle, SAP Tamino, or other vendors' database solution. Having the ability to connect and work on your database directly from the same tool you use to program is certainly convenient and saves money. The other more important aspect of having all these development capabilities integrated (can't use "bundled" or the DOJ might misinterpret what's going on here) is that they integrate—and well. Accessing the data store is only one step in building a database-driven application.

You need to create and modify tables, set constraints and relationships, and somehow tie your backend, middle-tier code, and user interface code together. You must also perform analysis and stress testing. Visual Studio .NET Enterprise Architect can do it all.

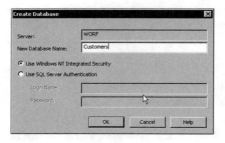

Figure 8.12

Creating a new database brings up a wizard to assist you.

This section takes a visual look at how you might create the database for a user registration system using some step-by-step figures.

After having created a user database from the *Server Explorer*, you need to create one or more database tables to store your information. This is easily done using the Server Explorer (see Figure 8.13).

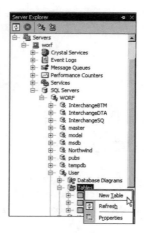

Figure 8.13

Create a new database table directly from the Server Explorer.

Once you have created a new table, you can now more easily create and edit columns of the table, including column names, types of data they will store, permissible lengths, and uniqueness constraints (see Figure 8.14).

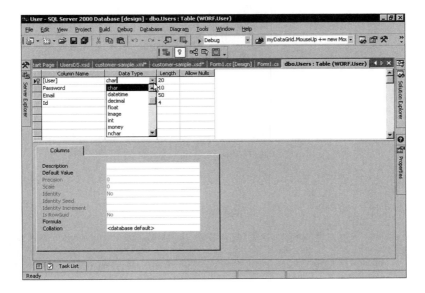

Figure 8.14

Create or edit a table in the database using the table editor.

In light of the fact that you are using a relational database it might prove helpful to create the appropriate relations (see Figure 8.15).

If your team is familiar with another database or database schema design tool, you will find the *Database Diagram* view familiar. It displays the tables graphically and shows the relationship through connecting lines. With this entity-relation diagram, you can simply right-click any table to bring up a context menu. This menu allows you to edit a table relationship, view or edit its constraint, and delete or create new columns. With similar ease, you can add or delete tables.

Unlike past iterations of Visual Studio, which were collections of useful tools that did not have a homogenous user interface or unified backend framework, the newest version is an integrated solution. Whether you choose to code in Microsoft Visual C++ or Microsoft C#, Microsoft Visual Basic .NET or JScript .NET, you use the *same exact* tool with the *same* interface and the *same* framework. This unified approach makes developing any solution, database driven or otherwise, infinitely less time consuming than working with multiple tools. Rest assured, although the user interface of Visual Studio .NET is intuitive and the dynamic help feature makes even development newbies feel at home, both the standard and enterprise versions are not a collection of lightweight tools added on to fill the *feature bucket*. These are hard-core tools, yet are easy to learn and use.

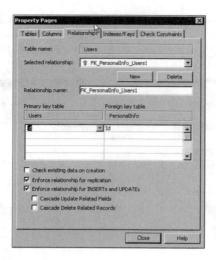

Figure 8.15

Creating relations is readily done using the relationships property sheet. There are also property sheets for setting table, column, index/keys, and constraints.

Web Services Support

.NET empowers its users to produce and consume Web services. Visual Studio .NET makes working with Web services no less difficult than writing traditional code. Similar to its integration of database services, accessing and integrating external services within your solution is straightforward.

If you simply choose to add a Web reference, a wizard comes to your aid (see Figure 8.16). This wizard makes it possible to type in the URL of a Web service if you know it or to search for services. Without going into the technical details, suffice it to say that the proxy to the Web service is added to your code and you can then call the service methods just as if you were calling your own class methods, framework classes/methods, or Windows APIs. It *is* that simple.

On the producer side of the Web services equation, if you want to expose an existing solution's functionality as a Web service or create a Web service from the ground up, it is no less troublesome. You simply code your solutions as you normally would and then mark each method you want to make visible externally as a Web Method. The tool will do the rest for you!

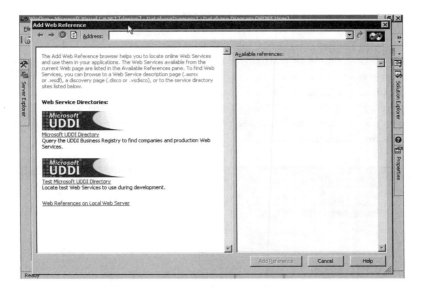

Figure 8.16

The Add Web Reference dialog box simplifies adding a Web service to your solution.

Granted, there are some design and implementation considerations to take into account, as mentioned in Chapter 7, "Web Services." However, the technical difference between what you need to do to create a Web service verses some other type of solution is negligible. This is thanks to the .NET Framework's design and implementation and to how well Visual Studio .NET leverages the infrastructure it targets.

Using Microsoft IntelliSense

You have already read something about Microsoft IntelliSense with relation to XML but it is not limited to writing XML. Visual Studio 6 also has Microsoft IntelliSense technology, but this version goes far beyond mere auto-indenting, syntax highlighting, and coding suggestions. Visual Studio .NET continuously validates everything you type in the code editor—everything. For example, if your code uses a class A and you mean to call a method doSomething using an instance of A, IntelliSense will bring up a context menu that shows you all versions of the method and the parameters that each version requires. As you continue typing, the context suggestion changes according to what you type, helping you to get it right the first time.

Dynamic Help

Aiding you further is the new dynamic help feature. It provides links to help topics based on the context of your cursor position. It continuously updates the links as you type, point, click, or do *anything* in Visual Studio .NET and, best of all, it does so in a non–obtrusive way by using a separate dedicated window pane. For example, Figure 8.17 shows the Dynamic Help system. It recognizes that a user interface button object was clicked and offers helpful links to the framework library documentation, sample code, and walkthroughs.

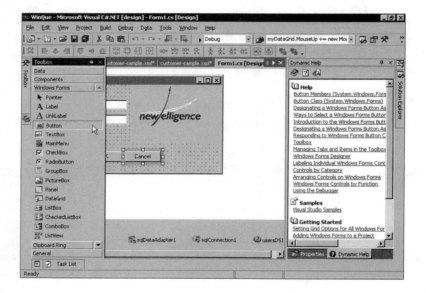

Figure 8.17

Dynamic help is available everywhere within the IDE, which makes learning and using Visual Studio .NET effortless.

Code Outlining

The last feature worth mentioning is code outlining. If you have ever written or read code, you know that files can get quite large and it becomes difficult to get an overview of the code. It also becomes difficult to navigate, because scrolling to a particular function point might mean navigating five pages of code to find what you seek. This scrolling back and forth between points in your code is a frustrating waste of time. But with outlining, you can collapse the code just like you do a tree view in Windows Explorer or in a Word document in the Outline view. There are various outlining options, such as *Collapse to Definitions*, which shows only the definitions in your code. You can also expand or collapse each definition individually or all at once (see Figure 8.18).

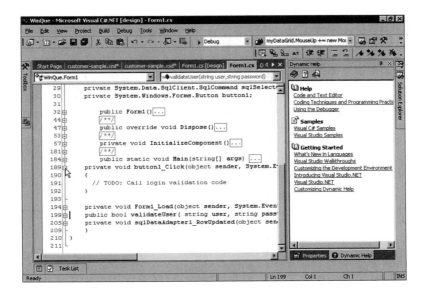

Figure 8.18

Code outlining allows you to collapse all or portions of code to definitions, which makes navigating and understanding large files simpler.

Case Studies on Visual Studio .NET

If you are not convinced that Visual Studio .NET offers you a lot of power and yet is easy to use, you might want to take a look at a few case studies Microsoft has made available on its Web site. Perhaps learning how other corporations are already putting .NET and the latest Microsoft development tools to work will help you make the decisions you need to make for your projects in the coming months. There are several case studies, including Continental Airlines, Scandinavian Airlines, Harris Interactive, CyberWatcher, and Zagat Survey.

The Continental Airlines case, for example, highlights how the company used Visual Studio .NET to build an information system capable of delivering up-to-date flight information available directly to its customers.

If you want to read more about any of these case studies, visit the Microsoft Web site: `http://msdn.microsoft.com/vstudio/prodinfo/casestudies/`.

Summary

Visual Studio .NET is a powerful successor to Visual Studio 6. In deference to it's heritage you will find that its new, more customizable user interface has a familiar feel to it. The wizards, IntelliSense, project templates and dynamic help system expedite becoming productive both with the tool and with .NET. The features Microsoft integrated to make building database, XML and Web service solutions possible make it likely that you will only need one tool—Visual Studio .NET—for most of your development needs, whether based on .NET or traditional Windows.

IV

.NET Meets the Enterprise Servers

Introducing .NET Enterprise Servers   9

Introducing .NET Enterprise Servers

Rounding out the .NET solution framework is the .NET Enterprise Servers, which is somewhat of a misnomer because there is no .NET-specific technology in them. As you learned in Chapter 4, "What Is .NET?," most of these servers were in production before the development of .NET, and the others are still in production. As such, it was simply impossible to build them using the framework. However, because these servers are Enterprise servers built atop the well-founded and understood COM/COM+ infrastructure introduced with NT/Windows 2000, they are solid server solutions that provide services that business solutions require. Figure 9.1 shows one way that.NET and the .NET Servers fit together.

.NET and the Enterprise Servers

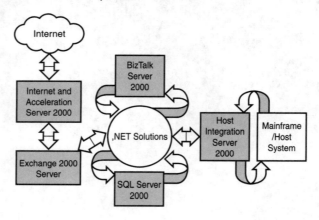

Figure 9.1

How the .NET Enterprise Servers and .NET fit together.

The fact that .NET framework includes excellent support for COM/COM+ through the COM Interop technologies helps make integrating the services of these servers more seamless. You can be sure that Microsoft will only continue to enhance their server offerings with regards to .NET in the future, as is exemplified by the forthcoming Windows .NET Server (the successor to Windows 2000 Server commonly known as "Whistler").

The following sections give you a short overview of business purpose of each of these servers and highlight some features that you might find useful.

BizTalk Server 2000

One of the more interesting servers in this family is the Microsoft BizTalk Server 2000, which was released just in time to qualify it for the "2000" designation.

You might also think of it as the most .NET of all the servers because of its tight integration and use of XML, XML Schema, and SOAP.

BizTalk is *the* integration server of the .NET platform. Actually, you might think of it as the only integration server, as this all-new Microsoft product has no real competition in its space. The server specializes in unifying the different information-exchange standards in use today, thus enabling corporations to tie all their processing resources into orchestrated workflows.

Note

BizTalk Server 2000 actually uses the older XML schema standard, called XML Data Reduced (XDR), because XML Schema (XSD) was not finalized at the time of development. XDR, on the other hand, is a Microsoft intermediary schema solution whose definition is unchanging. XSD has since become a candidate recommendation. You can expect that Microsoft will provide some kind of update to BizTalk Server 2000 or migration tool so that it can utilize the newer, stable-open standard.

Orchestrating Information

The concept of orchestrating information is core to BizTalk. Using a Microsoft Visio-based designer, you can link different platforms, applications, and services into workflow diagrams. The ability to do this with a drag-and-drop user interface in a collaborative manner empowers business analysts and developers to work together to quickly define business processes and integrate them with existing applications.

Messaging with Open Standards

Because of its business-document centricity and use of XML, BizTalk makes it possible to integrate dynamic business processes not only within your organization but also with partners or even across the Internet. The entire messaging engine is built on XML standards, thus making it possible to create mappings between documents in various formats. This makes document/information exchange between applications and services possible and consistent.

Although XML is used internally for all messaging, externally BizTalk can communicate not only using XML documents but also using two of the most popular electronic data interchange (EDI) standards: ANSI X12 and UN/EDIFACT (United Nations/Electronic Data Interchange for Administration, Commerce, and Transport). BizTalk supports integration with applications that communicate using these EDI standards, which makes it possible to communicate seamlessly with a variety of existing, deployed systems and partners.

BizTalk also supports several transport protocols including HTTP, HTTPS, Simple Mail Transfer Protocol (SMTP) and flat file transfers. This limitation is not restricting, however, as the server was designed to be extensible making it possible to overcome its out-of-the-box limitations. You can extend BizTalk by creating—and using—application integration components from Microsoft and third-parties or by integrating applications through the use of custom transport protocols.

Note

An example of an add-on that extends BizTalk is BizFTP, from newtelligence AG. This component enables BizTalk to use FTP, making it possible for you to use BizTalk with customers who require the use of "drop-off" document locations.

BizTalk is truly a revolutionary product and even in its first incarnation is a product you should consider if you are defining and integrating business processes or integrating services and applications. If you are interested in learning more about BizTalk, a definitive book on the topic is *BizTalk Server 2000: A Beginners Guide*, by Clemens F. Vasters (ISBN: 0072190116). Please note that, while the title says beginner, the power and flexibility that BizTalk brings to the table comes at the cost of some complexity.

SQL Server 2000

Microsoft SQL Server 2000 is a relational database that competes squarely against IBM DB/2 and Oracle Oracle9i. As the successor to SQL Server 7, SQL Server 2000 builds on the ease of use of its predecessor and offers further performance improvements.

This latest version of SQL Server continues to hold the title of the world's fastest relational database system. In the Transaction Processing Performance Council (TPC) TPC-C test, SQL Server took the number one and number three spots for performance.

Note

The TPC-C test simulates real-world use of a database and involves a mix of different transactions processed in parallel or queued for execution. For more information, refer to the Transaction Processing Performance Council Web site at www.tpc.org.

Reliability and Scalability

In addition to speed, reliability and scalability are important features for a relational database. To this end, SQL Server 2000 offers you the ability to take advantage of multiprocessor server. SQL Server 2000 can take advantage of up to 32 processor on a symmetric multiprocessor (SMP) system with up to 64 Megabytes (MB) of memory. Additionally, you can distribute the database over multiple machines to help manage the processing if your business requires it. Lastly, the reliability of SQL Server 2000 is increased because it has failover clustering, which is the ability of setting up several servers that effectively act as one so that if a system fails another can seamlessly take over. This failover helps keep your data—and business—up and running at all times.s

Data Warehousing

SQL Server comes with Analysis Services (formerly OLAP Services), which offers businesses integrated online analytical processing (OLAP) and data-mining capabilities. You can use OLAP to perform rapid, sophisticated analysis on large and complex data sets. This makes it easier for you to turn your data into information that you can leverage. The data-mining functionality gives you another way to get hold of the big picture by helping you reveal patterns and trends otherwise hidden in large amounts of data. By efficiently analyzing your existing data, you can use this functionality to predict future trends.

Using SQL Server 2000 to mine you data is even easier now with the improvements in its natural language query facilities. This English query feature makes retrieving your data more intuitive—and more productive.

e-Commerce

SQL Server 2000 complements both BizTalk Server 2000 and .NET with its XML-enabled relational database engine. Not only are you able to store XML documents—data—relationally but you also can specify that the results of your query be returned as an XML document. This simplifies back-end system integration and allows seamless data transfer, even across firewalls. It also makes it easier to design and implement a Web service that requires querying your data store because, as you know, Web services use XML. SQL Server 2000 integrates especially well with .NET applications thanks to ADO.NET, which can communicate its data as XML as well as use XML internally. Furthermore, ADO.NET comes with two sets of data access classes: one for any OLE DB provider and one optimized for SQL Server 2000.

Because you can access SQL Server 2000 can via HTTP or HTTPS, it makes using the Web a viable option. The fact that you can choose the unsecured HTTP protocol or its secure counterpart, HTTPS, with no additional programming enables you to make the decision if speed or security is paramount.

There are countless features in SQL Server 2000 that it makes no sense to delve into here. However, the few highlights mentioned here should help you understand how it can become part of your e-commerce or internal solutions. Certainly its XML capabilities make it a logical choice for storing Web service data and earn it consideration when looking at partnering a database with BizTalk Server 2000.

Exchange 2000 Server

Microsoft Exchange Server 2000 is an e-mail, messaging, and collaboration server created to take full advantage of the capabilities of Windows 2000 it benefits from its complete integration with Active Directory Services. Exchange Server 2000 is the first application to offer unified management of all messaging, collaboration, and network capabilities and resources. The result is that Exchange can store and deliver more than just e-mail messages, making online collaboration and sending and receiving instant messages possible.

As you might know, instant messaging has grown in popularity and is maturing from a consumer oriented chat application to one increasingly used in a business environment for impromptu "meetings." The short-coming of this technology is that it is still mostly a consumer oriented application that offers little in the way of management. Exchange 2000, however, takes the chat-pardigm to the office by letting you offer messaging from within your company rather than using third-party hosted solutions. By using Exchange for such services, you also benefit from the fact that the conversations are stored in-house making it possible to return to the information conveyed if necessary—like your email today.

Exchange 2000 is truly an information server and because it is designed for the enterprise, you can rely on its stability. It appears that Microsoft has gone through lengths to improve stability, performance, and scalability of Exchange 2000 Server.

Web Storage and Native XML Support

Like SQL Server 2000 and BizTalk Server 2000, there is no .NET in the product but there is plenty of "Net" in it. Exchange is the third enterprise server well versed in XML and supporting various XML technologies. Underlying the entire system is the Microsoft Web Storage System, which serves as the single place to create, store, access, and share all the knowledge accumulated in your company. The data residing in the Web Storage System is stored natively in XML and you can access it using HTTP. This simplifies storing, retrieving, sharing, and representing information between Exchange and other applications. Thinking back to the discussion of ADO.NET and XML, you can imagine that creating .NET solutions that leverage features of Exchange 2000 are significantly eased.

This version of Exchange also comes with native support for Web Distributed Authoring and Versioning (WebDAV) and Active Server Pages (ASP). Combined, these features make Exchange 2000 the ideal platform upon which to build a new generation of applications that handle day-to-day business tasks and manage the flow of ideas and information.

Anywhere, Anytime Communication

Exchange 2000 Server promotes the .NET philosophy of anywhere, anytime communication. With this version of Exchange, you can access your e-mail anywhere, anytime using the enhanced Microsoft Outlook Web Access (OWA). You can also work with your calendar and contacts using your Web browser. Additionally, its real-time collaboration and instant messaging features respond to the increased demand for ways to save money by reducing travel budgets.

Host Integration Server 2000

Microsoft Host Integration Server facilitates connecting legacy systems to current client/server, Web-based or .NET-based application solutions. As its name states, it is targeted at integration. It's the glue that binds today with yesterday.

The server includes bridging technologies and Web-deployable 3270 and 5250 clients, direct Message Queuing (also known as MSMQ) integration with IBM MQSeries, security integration, and support for distributed transactions. These distributed transactions enlist the IBM customer interface control system (CICS) and the information management system (IMS) as well as Microsoft COM+ resources.

Internet Security and Acceleration Server 2000

Microsoft Internet Security and Acceleration (ISA) Server 2000 is the successor to Microsoft Proxy 2.0 and provides secure, fast, and manageable Internet connectivity. It builds on Microsoft Windows 2000 security and directory for policy-based security, acceleration, and management of internetworking.

Microsoft Proxy 2.0 offered a simple to manage, solid proxy solution to maximize performance of your corporate Internet connection. It also offered a reasonable amount of security with its limited abilities to restrict external access to your internal network. It's predecessor, however, takes a giant leap ahead in both categories.

The biggest improvement may come from its extensible firewall features that let you set security on a variety of levels including packet-, circuit-, and application-level traffic screening. It also features integrated virtual private networking (VPN) which helps secure communication between your office and remote locations, such as workers that log-in from home.

Using the improved Web caching features, you can maximize performance and save network bandwidth resources by storing and serving locally cached Web content. This allows employees to work faster and reduces costs because less bandwidth is needed to serve up Web pages.

Application Center 2000

Microsoft Application Center 2000 empowers both developers and administrators to deploy and operate applications. It is designed to ease managing groups (or farms) of computers, enables you to cluster servers together so that they perform as one (also known as software scaling or scaling out), and helps create fault tolerance because of the redundancy clustering offers.

Commerce Server 2000

Microsoft Commerce Server 2000, the successor to Microsoft Site Server, is an e-commerce solution. It is designed to make producing, managing and deploying e-commerce sites easier.

Commerce Server 2000 comes with an application framework that includes user management, a product catalog system, and a targeting system (for personalizing user experiences). It also features business-processing pipelines, which allow you to lie out and then customize your business processes like a workflow. Some customizable pipelines include an order pipeline, a direct mail pipeline, and a content-selection pipeline.

Internally Commerce Server 2000 communicates in XML, facilitating information sharing and making integration with BizTalk Server 2000, SQL Server 2000, Exchange Server 2000 and the other .NET Servers easier. Because Commerce Server 2000 was available prior to .NET, it relies on ASP (Active Server Pages) rather than ASP.NET; however, considering the ability of ASP.NET to server ASP pages this presents little-to-no problem and makes it an ideal candidate for integration into a .NET solution.

Mobile Information 2001 Server

Microsoft Mobile Information 2001 Server is the platform for extending the reach of Microsoft .NET enterprise applications, enterprise data, and intranet content into the realm of the mobile user. It helps deliver on the .NET vision of "any time, any place and on any device" by bringing the usefulness of the corporate intranet to the latest generation of mobile devices. This makes it possible for you to securely access e-mail, contacts, calendar, tasks, or any intranet application in real time.

Like its server sibling, Exchange 2000, Mobile Information 2001 Server comes with a specialized Outlook access client, Outlook Mobile Access (OMA). OMA is the mobile portal experience for browsing and receiving notifications from Outlook. It enables you to format messages, create secure message forwarding, and make corporate information accessible via a mobile phone, an alpha-numeric pager, or a text-enabled mobile device.

SharePoint Portal Server 2001

Microsoft SharePoint Portal Server 2001 is a flexible portal solution that lets you easily find, share, and publish information. Designed to facilitate information exchange within a business, it lets you create a Web portal from which people can easily share documents using a Web browser. However, SharePoint is not just a portal builder because it comes with a complete document management solution that makes it easier to use existing information and facilitates capturing new information. The advanced document-management features include coordinated locking, versioning, and publishing. In recognition that more information is not necessarily better information, SharePoint takes the concept of a "digital dashboard" and enables you to create customized views of your corporate data. Instead of clicking through an ever-expanding hierarchical tree of folders to navigate to the document you need, you can create one or more views of each document or document store that makes logical sense. While you can create and publish these views for others in the organization, you can also permit each user to customize his/her dashboard to best fit his/her needs. SharePoint Portal Server's effectiveness is further increased because of its integration with Office and Outlook/Exchange.

Summary

Although the .NET Enterprise Servers are not built using NET technology, they all utilize various Web-based technologies, such as HTTP, HTML, and XML. Because these technologies are also the foundation technologies of .NET, you should not be surprised that .NET and the .NET Enterprise Servers complement one another well and integrate proficiently. The common lineage of these Microsoft technologies makes them a natural choice when looking to augment your .NET solutions.

Moving Forward

Migration Paths— From Anywhere to .NET

Producing native .NET applications rather than traditional solutions has many advantages. However, you might have a good reason not to build a solution from the ground up using .NET at this time. Consider the following scenarios in which you might not want to produce a completely new .NET-based solution:

- Perhaps you want to take a wait-and-see approach before building a new solution using new technology.
- Maybe you don't have the time, money, or inclination to rewrite existing applications.
- Perhaps you or your team doesn't yet have the expertise to fully leverage .NET—or the time to learn it adequately.
- You might be invested heavily in your current solution(s) and want to continue to benefit from them.

Whatever the scenario, it's important to know that there are many migration paths to .NET, from which you can pick and choose. Each method has its own positive aspects; it depends on your perspective.

Support for C/C++

Because there is a huge installed base of both C/C++ and Visual Basic 6 programmers and programs, you should welcome the news that you don't have to discard the solutions or retrain yourself or your developers to begin migrating to .NET.

The power of C/C++ comes from its freedom to get "down to the metal." As you may know, this is also its liability. For example, the capability to do just anything and everything with computer memory using C++ makes it possible to do anything, including introduce serious bugs that threaten stability and security. C++ does nothing to manage memory except delegate the responsibility to you, the programmer. This is diametrically opposed to the common language runtime, which manages memory for you. In a sense, C# is the managed answer to C++; it has almost identical syntax and grammar but provides more guidance by effectively restricting your possibilities. The tradeoff between freedom of expression and stability, however, is not a great one and you probably will welcome the features C# introduces, which include much more than simply limiting how you use memory in your programs (but that is not a topic for this book).

If you have an existing solution that you want to run under the .NET Platform or utilize from a .NET solution, you have two choices. You can run your existing C++ solution as "unmanaged" or migrate it using C++ managed extensions.

The easiest solution is obviously to run "as is," which means the solution is "unmanaged." Running your program as unmanaged code does allow you to call it from future .NET applications and visa versa. The downside is that your C++

solution loses all the benefits that runtime management provides, most notably memory management.

The second option is to retrofit your existing C++ solutions so that they can be managed. You can do this by including several special directives in your code that instruct the (Visual Studio .NET) compiler to wrap your solution in a manner that the common language runtime can manage it. For example, by prefacing your classes with the __gc keyword, you instruct the runtime to garbage-collect the class. This keyword also informs the runtime that it should manage memory for arrays and pointers. Of course, if you use managed extensions there is more work than simply adding a few keywords. Because the runtime handles disposing of memory, you must also make sure that your C++ code no longer explicitly does this.

Support for COM in .NET

There is a *lot* of software in use today built using COM/COM+; Windows itself uses it extensively. As such, it is little wonder that the .NET team went through pains to make sure .NET can interact with existing COM-based solutions. Given that the .NET enterprise servers are COM/COM+ based, this also makes it possible to fully exploit the services they provide. Another motivation to make .NET interoperate with the COM world is because COM software will continue to exist for some time, as will development of COM-based solutions. No one expects the migration to .NET to happen overnight.

For these reasons, the COM Interop/PInvoke technologies exist. These include tools to import COM-type libraries and can generate callable runtime wrappers that .NET interfaces with when using COM objects. There is also a COM-callable wrapper that permits COM objects to call .NET objects. Although the details of COM Interop/PInvoke are outside the scope of this book, you need only be aware that Microsoft has included the means for COM- and .NET-based solutions to interoperate. Obviously, this gives you the capability to migrate your COM solutions gradually to .NET or to maintain existing COM based solutions while building new features and solutions using .NET.

From Visual Basic 6 to VB.NET

Another way .NET offers "backward" compatibility is by helping to migrate Visual Basic 6 programs to the new version, Visual Basic .NET. Although the .NET version tries to maintain the Visual Basic heritage, the .NET version is fundamentally different in some ways. First and foremost, Visual Basic .NET is a fully objected-oriented language. Unlike Visual Basic, where primitive types were not actually objects, in the .NET version they are. Previous versions of the language also did not support implementation inheritance, so you could not, for example, create a standard form template for your company with a specialized look and feel and then derive from it; now you can. There are additional changes that are significant enough to prevent you from compiling and running existing Visual Basic code on the .NET platform.

But all hope is not lost. Microsoft recognizes that the Visual Basic community is one of the biggest development communities and there is a huge number of applications written in Visual Basic. To ease the transition to .NET, Visual Studio .NET comes with a wizard that helps you port your solutions to Visual Basic .NET. Essentially, you feed the wizard your existing code and it outputs a new version choc-full of changes. Wherever it can determine which changes to make, it does so. However, being that it is an automated process that attempts to determine the best alterations, it certainly is not fail-proof. To counter unfortunate alterations, the wizard generates a log of changes and comments the code so that you can review what it has done. Also, in the instances where it cannot conclude what to do, it flags the code with a warning comment to bring your attention to it. Granted, a complex Visual Basic 6 program *will* need work to make it run on the new runtime (possibly even more work than a C++ application and certainly more than using COM); however the important point is a path exists for your existing VB solutions.

Java User Migration Path (JUMP) to Microsoft .NET

The final aspect of migration that you will read about is the Java User Migration Path (JUMP) to .NET. JUMP is part of two pronged strategy to help you secure your past investment in Java:

- Visual J#
- Java migration wizard

Visual J#

Microsoft Visual J# is the successor to the Microsoft Visual J++. Visual J# integrates fully into Visual Studio .NET so that you can benefit from all the development environment advancements the tool offers. Visual J++ developers will find that using Visual J# little challenge. It is obvious that Microsoft's goal is to help you maximize your investment in J++ and Java skills and increase the longevity of your J++ and Java based solutions.

Visual J# includes a migration wizard similar to that available Visual Basic 6. Once you you migrate to J# your solution becomes a first class citizen of .NET. While this means that it will no longer run on the Java Virtual Machine, it means that it is native to .NET and all the benefits of the .NET Platform. You can, for example, leverage non-Java–specific technologies such as ADO.NET and ASP.NET. You can also easily Web service–enable your application or integrate solutions written in other languages, such as Visual Basic .NET and C#.

Note

Visual J++ was not originally part of Visual Studio .NET but was made available later. This demonstrates both the extensibility of Visual Studio .NET and the commitment by Microsoft to help customers migrate to .NET

Migration Wizard—Java to C#

Although Visual J# lets you prolong and enhance your investment in your Java based skills and solutions, it is not the only migration path available to you. Microsoft has also created migration wizard that translates Java code into C# code. This automated process not only handles the translation but substitutes Java library calls to corresponding .NET Framework library classes. As with the Visual Basic .NET wizard, code that the wizard cannot resolve is conveniently flagged and presented to you for manual translation.

This two pronged approach to helping you move from Java to .NET attests to Microsoft's commitment to your migration issues.

Summary

.NET is here to stay. However, the history of COBOL is any indication of the longevity of solutions—and certainly many thought COBOL would be long dead by now—COM, Visual Basic 6, Java and C++ will remain for some time. Unlike many new development platforms that require you to do away with the past, .NET makes it possible to embrace the past (at least when it comes to COM/COM+ and C++). COM interoperability is built directly into the .NET framework (in the `System.Runtime.InteropServices` namespace), as is the capability to either wrap up C++ programs so they run managed or execute them as they are. In this way, .NET preserves your past investments well into the future and gives you the power to evaluate and decide which solutions to use and how fast you want to migrate.

11

Summarizing the Key Benefits of .NET

You have hopefully gained at least a foundation of knowledge about the Microsoft .NET Platform from the previous chapters. The goal of the book, as you well know, is to give you a better idea of what this "thing" .NET is all about and how it differs from existing architectural solutions. It is meant as an orientation to information technology managers and I hope it transfers enough of technology from a bird's eye view to convey the philosophy and potential of .NET. This book is certainly only a starting point meant to help you decide if you or your team should investigate the technology further. And as you might have gleaned, there is a *lot* under the hood to learn if you decide to actually develop solutions using the framework, tools, or servers. This journey only scratches the surface.

The framework itself—the core of .NET—needs a book, if not more, unto itself. Chapter 5, "Introducing the Class Library," didn't cover much about the new data access technology of .NET, called ADO.NET or the Windows Forms library that Microsoft has introduced to unify the different Windows programming models (MFC, VB, and so on) to make developing in any language more simple and consistent. There are countless classes in .NET that make things happen, such as remoting and reflection. These classes are both interesting and important but are not within the scope here.

What you should take away from this book is an appreciation for the framework—which is without a doubt—a work of technical design elegance. Framework is an easy-to-understand, well-organized class library whose intuitively laid out namespaces facilitate development for both new-comers to Windows and developers in general. When you consider that there are somewhere around 6,000 classes in the .NET framework, you quickly learn to appreciate such clear organization. It makes both getting accustomed to the library and using it on a daily basis quicker and easier. There are hurdles to using .NET, especially for those developers coming from a non-object-oriented camp, but the result far outweighs the "startup cost."

Note

The huge number of classes that comprise the framework need not scare you as there is much redundancy in classes due to object-oriented nature of the library—classes inherit from one another.

Although the framework library is the cleanest design I've seen since Borland's OWL, there is certainly a learning curve. It might be easy to get going but doing the more complicated things takes a deeper understanding and that takes time. Furthermore, using a development tool such as Visual Studio .NET makes the transition that much less painless. Let me just say, "This tool is cool!"

Although pundits of Microsoft claim that .NET is just a new technology and development platform to lock people into Windows, its foundation on open standards counters such arguments. Furthermore, don't forget that the core of the framework and the language with which it was written, C#, were submitted to ECMA for standardization. Microsoft truly wants to become an enterprise player and in the face of the open source/Linux movement and its gaining popularity, I firmly believe that Microsoft is trying in earnest to be more open, without giving the farm away.

Common Language Runtime

This brings up the second big benefit of .NET: the common language runtime. The .NET runtime is an amazing piece of work. The potential of writing your code in any language you want and running it in the same execution environment and potentially on any operating system is more than Java (or the JVM) ever strived to be or will become. Adding to this feat is the ability to integrate applications or application components written in different languages or technologies (such as COM/COM+) which addresses development resource and legacy issues head-on.

Admittedly there is a downside to having the flexibility of using "any" language. You might not want to mix the languages used in a project or within your development team because it can make code management more difficult later on. For example, if you develop some code in JScript.NET and other code in C# and then the C# developers leave, the JScript team is left to learn C# *and* decipher the existing code. But this is an issue that you can avoid with proper management. On the upside of such flexibility, consider a scenario in which you have a limited budget and your existing team has separate language skills. You can utilize them immediately with .NET—there is no down time having required to synchronize everyone with one language. Your team only needs to be familiar with the framework library to get up and running.

Web Services

Web services is a new phenomenon that is taking the industry and especially the trade press by storm. It is reminiscent of XML, which has existed since circa 1998, but only took flight in late 1999–2000. Suddenly everything was XML. But the fact is, XML has proven itself exactly the way everyone had hoped—if not more—and Web services, which are built atop XML technologies, seem as if they will do the same.

The idea to offer your solution as a service, deliverable any time, anywhere, and on any device, *is* tantalizing. Not only can Web services facilitate the transfer of data within an organization, but they offer new ways to fill that possibly dot-com busted revenue stream. Suddenly you can take a service that wouldn't work well over the Internet because user intervention was always needed and make it do so without the user getting involved. Additionally you can integrate Web services into traditional applications as discussed in Chapter 3, "Why .NET?". You can build solutions from these new Web components or differentiate versions in your product line by making some features pay services. Certainly the rollout of Microsoft's HailStorm at Professional Developers Conference (PDC) will bring with it some novel approaches to using Web services.

Integration Existing Solutions

But .NET is not only about using Web services to offer new solutions. It also allows you to integrate existing solutions. You can also expose legacy applications as Web services. For example, you might create a light middle-tier that integrates with the back-end system and exposes its features as one or more services via the Web. You might choose to do this as a free service, a pay service to the public, or simply to empower partnering companies.

When leveraging existing Windows solutions or migrating them to new technologies, .NET shines. The COM interoperability that the framework offers—the ability to use COM objects—should prove attractive to you if you have already invested heavily in COM/COM+ technology and want to reap rewards from those investments as you make a transition to .NET. Microsoft really should get kudos for finding a way to breathe new life into COM/COM+ because, face it, at eight years old, COM is ancient by technology life-span terms!

The great benefit of .NET is that by using ASP.NET or the Microsoft Mobile Information Server 2001, you can also deliver Web-based applications to any device—without writing special code to do so! If your company has workers in the field—such as sales people—you can imagine the benefit of them getting up-to-the-minute information, wherever they are. On the other hand, the back office certainly would not mind knowing that a sale has been booked immediately rather than a week later. Again, .NET proves it is a facilitator.

Assemblies Ease Deployment

If your organization is like most, you have Windows deployed to some extent—either for back-end processing, development, or for the front office. In all of these cases you have undoubtedly experienced "DLL Hell" in one way or shape and it probably took much of your time or someone else's to rectify. Again, .NET comes to the rescue because .NET deployment modules (assemblies) do not pollute your system or require registration of COM objects in the Windows Registry. This means you don't have to destabilize your system by installing the demo of Tetris (or the latest accounting software). You also can now deploy different versions of the same application side-by-side. This is a great comfort, for example, if you are using the current version of an application but want to evaluate the usefulness of a new version on the same machine. Another scenario in which this comes into play is when you must keep the old version running for some period of time as you transition to the new solution, as is often the case in some data-sensitive businesses. With .NET solutions, this is a no-brainer.

The benefits of .NET are many. In my opinion, if you are currently developing Windows solutions, there should be little question about using .NET. If your company currently uses Java, the transition to C# will prove rather straightforward. Both are object-oriented languages with their roots in C++. But the performance gain you get with C# on .NET is noticeable. Additionally, .NET is built from the ground with Web services in mind—it isn't an add-on like Java APIs for XML Processing—and uses HTTP, XML, and SOAP natively—again, there are no bridging or layers added to make this possible.

Hopefully you have gained a broad understanding of what .NET is, recognize the vision driving it and see how it addresses the challenges that face developers and end-users in a pre-.NET world. The potential to build new applications, using your choice of language with one unified framework and development paradigm is enticing. Microsoft has delivered all this and the ease to build better, more interoperable desktop applications, server solutions, Web applications and Web services.

.NET is what development should be like—and will become.

Index

X-Z

QUE® has .NET Covered!

Microsoft announced in 2000 that the company's new initiative, the .NET framework, would revolutionize how computer applications were programmed by developers and accessed by users forever. Since that announcement Que has signed bestselling authors to our most popular book series to bring our readers the best and most comprehensive introductions to .NET and the soon to be released Visual Studio.NET. Because of the interactivity among the different programming languages that make up Visual Studio.NET, more and more programmers who focused on one or two languages in the past are upgrading their skills to include multiple languages. Whether you are looking to learn an entirely new language or to update your skills in the new .NET environment, Que has the books and the information you need.

ASP.NET

ASP.NET by Example
ISBN: 0789725622
Author: Steve Smith
Price: $29.99
464 pages

Steve Smith, is a Managing Consultant and Internet Specialist for Software Architects, Inc., a Chicago-based consulting firm with offices in over a dozen US cities. In his spare time, Steve runs the #1 ASP.NET community site, ASPAlliance.com, and maintains a column there with dozens of articles on ASP and ASP.NET. He has also written a number of articles for ASPToday.com and continues to work as a technical reviewer for WROX, Prentice Hall, and QUE. Steve has an MCSE+Internet (4.0) certification and previously completed the MCSD. He is also a graduate of Ohio State University with a degree in Computer Science Engineering. His computer experience prior to .NET was mainly focused on ASP, VB, SQL Server, and COM+.

ASP developers need to understand how ASP.NET can help them solve business problems better than any prior product. *ASP.NET by Example* is designed to provide a "crash course" on ASP.NET and quickly help the reader start using this new technology. As part of the *By Example* series, this book approaches ASP.NET in an easy-to-use tutorial way, giving the reader a much faster and more interactive learning experience than the traditional reference book. By building the sample applications explained in the book, readers will learn how to create custom ASP.NET controls, how to use ADO+ objects in ASP, and how to deploy and manage applications. *ASP.NET by Example* also provides tools and information needed to migrate old ASP files to the new platform, saving developers significant time and money. As an added feature the author has included multiple case studies on how ASP.NET is used in e-commerce applications.

OTHER ASP.NET TITLES

Special Edition Using ASP.NET	Richard Leinecker	0789725606	$49.99

Que is excited to publish the only book on the market to explain application prototyping with Visual Basic. Visual Basic is the ultimate rapid application development (RAD) tool in software programming, saving companies time, cost as well as reducing the risk when building complex applications. By building a prototype a development team can access a project's feasibility, define functionality and user interfaces, and identify potential problems long before the first line of code is written.

Prototyping with Visual Basic teaches readers what kind of prototypes to build for various applications as well as how to take the next step towards building a fully functional application. The author, Rod Stephens, explains the benefits of prototyping using real-world examples from his twenty years in programming.

Prototyping with Visual Basic
ISBN: 0789725789
Author: Rod Stephens
Price: $39.99
432 pages

Microsoft's .NET initiative created drastic changes in the Visual Studio line of products, and as a result a lot of Visual Basic developers feel like they are beginners all over again. *Special Edition Using Visual Basic.NET* will offer in-depth explorations of new features so that both experienced programmers and novices will feel comfortable making the transition to .NET. Although a major portion of the book is devoted to Internet applications, the book covers more general topics than many other books. Features of Visual Basic that will be explained include database access, controls, and best coding and practices. These features will be explored in detail, with extensive use of example programs and screen captures.

Special Edition Using Visual Basic.NET is a comprehensive resource that will help readers leverage the exciting new features of Visual Basic.NET as well as port their skills to the new .NET development environment. The authors, Jeff Spotts and Brian Siler, are recognized Visual Basic experts who have crafted a book that blends a fundamental understanding of VB.NET with hard-earned experience in the field. With the new ntegrated programming language approach .NET brings to the table for programmers, this book contains extensive coverage of using Visual Basic with the other Microsoft Visual Studio.NET languages and software including ADO+, Visual C#.NET, Visual Fox Pro 7, Visual C++.NET, and ASP.NET.

Special Edition Using Visual Basic.NET
ISBN: 078972572X
Author: Jeff Spotts and Brian Siler
Price: $39.99
896 pages

OTHER VISUAL BASIC .NET TITLES

Windows Game Programming with Visual Basic and DirectX	Wayne Freeze	0789725924	$39.99
Visual Basic.NET by Example	Donald & Oancea	0789725835	$29.99

Visual C++.NET

Kate Gregory is a founding partner of Gregory Consulting Limited (www.gregcons.com,), which has been providing consulting and development services throughout North America since 1986. She is the author of numerous books for Que, including three previous editions of *Special Edition Using Visual C++*. She speaks at conferences such as Developer Days on Microsoft technologies, XML, and the .NET initiative. Kate is in demand as a speaker because she combines a solid technical understanding of her material with warmth, humor, and her own development experience. She teaches and develops courses for IBM, CDI Corporate Education, and ThinkPath. Her topics include XML, XSLT, UML, Object-Oriented Analysis and Design, C++, Visual C++, Java, and the Internet.

Special Edition Using Visual C++.NET
ISBN: 0789724669
Author: Kate Gregory
Price: $49.99
900 pages

Special Edition Using Visual C++.NET is a comprehensive resource to help readers leverage the exciting new features of Visual C++.NET as well as port their existing skills to the new .NET development environment. The book shows how both Win32 and .NET applications work, not only instructing the reader in the use of Microsoft's Visual C++ wizards, but also showing what the wizards create. A variety of programming tasks from simple dialog boxes to database and Internet programming are included. Because of the new .NET platform developers in any of 17 languages (including Visual C++) will use the same class libraries to construct high-performance applications. *Special Edition Using Visual C++.NET* will not only cover the new version of the software but also how to get maximum programming results from combining several languages into one project. Related technologies such as XML and XSLT are also covered, along with integrating Visual C++ code with Visual Basic and C# code.

Visual C#.NET

Visual C#.NET is a completely new language engineered by Microsoft to encompass the strengths and fix the problems of C, C++, and Visual Basic. *Special Edition Using Visual C#.NET* will provide a comprehensive training and reference resource to readers. The book includes extensive information on C# and how it works with the NGWS runtime environment, Visual C++.NET, Java, Jscript, Visual Basic.NET, ADO+, ASP.NET plus much more. As part of the *Special Edition Using* series, the book is a comprehensive training guide with multiple programming examples and projects as well as a complete reference to C# and its intricacies. Because it is a book written for IT professionals and students, special emphasis is put on troubleshooting, debugging, and hands-on learning. The authors of *SE Using Visual C#.NET* come to Que from NIIT, a global, multifaceted organization based in India specializing in software development, education, training and e-business solutions. NIIT has the world's largest educational multimedia software development facility with a team of over 700 instructional design professionals and provides computer training at 1,970 learning centers in 26 different countries including the United States. NIIT has received many awards for their excellence in training and programming including the "Best Training Award" from Microsoft.

Special Edition Using Visual C#.NET
ISBN: 0789725754
Author: NIIT
Price: $49.99
800 pages

OTHER C#.NET TITLES

Visual C#.NET by Example	Alan Eliason	0789725592	$34.99